D0518672

700040742672

A CLASSIC TREAT REINVENTED

DOUGHNUTS

A CLASSIC TREAT REINVENTED

DOUGHNUTS

60 easy, delicious recipes

ROSIE REYNOLDS

CONTENTS

This is a collection of 60 recipes to celebrate the doughnut, whether it be round or ringed. There are loads of flavour combinations here, inspired by my favourite childhood treats and the many yummy things I've eaten along the way since then – it's surprising how many things taste even better when turned into a doughnut!

For a long time doughnuts were, for me, either the piping hot, sugar-rolled rings eaten on New Brighton Beach, or the sweet treats bought in multi-packs at the supermarket by my mum to keep my sisters and me quiet while she shopped! More recently, I've indulged in some more extravagant flavours offered by a few of London's top foodie destinations: beef-cheek doughnuts anyone?

Most countries have some variety of doughnut in their regional cuisine, from the Italian bombolone, stuffed with everything from custard to chocolate and hazelnut spread, to the Indian gulab jamun, often fragranced with rose water but here soaked in spiced Chai tea syrup. It turns out the doughnut is much more versatile and interesting than I previously thought...

If you're put off by the idea of fried dough, well, try baked doughnuts instead. Freshly made and either drizzled with icing or brushed with a little melted butter and rolled in sugar, they are absolutely delicious. There are fried doughnuts here, too, because homemade and eaten still warm, they are really, really good – and frying with a vat of oil isn't as scary as it sounds.

What about doughnut cakes? They look like a doughnut but taste like a cake! I've made these with yogurt and oil instead of butter, which gives them a dense texture that holds a good ringed shape.

Cupcake towers and croquembouche have been around for a while, so what about a doughnut tower instead? Baked, stacked and drizzled with chocolate, they make a great birthday cake alternative – try Rocky Mountain in chapter 4.

There's even a chapter on virtuous doughnuts. Worry not, I'm not suggesting you fill deep-fried fresh air with jam. Rather, these doughnuts have a bit of fruit or veg, use wholemeal flour or are gluten- or dairy-free – they still pack a flavour punch.

Doughnuts have been over-looked for too long and it's time to give them a rebranding. They are so versatile – whatever tickles your fancy, there should be a doughnut for everyone in this book. Enjoy!

Rosie Reynolds

WHAT IS A DOUGHNUT?

Typically, doughnuts are made from enriched, yeasted dough, which is then often deep-fried, rolled in sugar and filled. You'll see that throughout this book I've used a basic enriched dough, 'The Classic', as the starting point for most of the doughnut recipes. I suggest you make The Classic first, get used to the method and then try the rest of the recipes.

There are other variations here – some arguably not doughnut-like at all e.g choux buns and doughnut cakes. Choux buns look like posh doughnuts and the pastry is made using basic ingredients and a not-too-difficult method. You don't even have to get your hands dirty: water and butter are brought to the boil, plain flour is added then eggs are beaten in. Eggs cause the pastry to puff up rather like a doughnut, and choux pastry can also be baked or fried. Do not be afraid of choux pastry, give it a try.

Whichever doughnut you decide to make, the most important thing is to have fun and give it a go.

USEFUL EQUIPMENT

Here's a list of equipment you will need to make the doughnuts in this book:

LARGE MIXING BOWL
SMALL BOWLS – for icings and fillings
MEASURING JUG
SET OF DIGITAL SCALES
SET OF MEASURING SPOONS – ranging from ¼ teaspoon to 1 tablespoon
SET OF ROUND CUTTERS (not essential)
WOODEN SPOON, TEASPOONS, DESSERTSPOON AND A SLOTTED METAL
   SPOON (for frying)
ELECTRIC HAND WHISK (makes beating so much quicker)
SHARP KNIFE, A ROUND-ENDED KNIFE AND A SMALL SERRATED KNIFE
SMALL AND MEDIUM-SIZED SAUCEPAN
COUPLE OF BAKING SHEETS AND LOTS OF NON-STICK BAKING PAPER
KITCHEN/SUGAR THERMOMETER – very important to achieve the correct
   temperature of the frying oil

DOUGHNUT TIN — available online and from cook's shops, these have six ringed holes perfect for making ringed doughnuts and doughnut cakes.

DOUGHNUT MAKER — not essential for this book, but a lot of fun! Available online and from cook's shops, doughnut makers are easy to use, producing high yields of tasty, pretty little doughnuts really quickly. Throughout this book, recipes for doughnuts that can be made with a doughnut maker will state 'Makes 6 large or 30 mini' doughnuts. Follow the method on page 88, as well as the manufacturer's instructions for your doughnut maker to make 30 mini doughnuts.

PIPING BAG AND NOZZLES — 0.5cm round, 1cm round and star-shaped, and 1.5 cm round and star-shaped nozzles are used in this book.

BASIC INGREDIENTS

The great thing about these doughnuts is that they are made with accessible, easy-to-find ingredients. The most out-there ingredient used is pumpkin purée, which can be found in lots of supermarkets especially around Halloween.

Most of the doughnuts here are made using an enriched dough: butter, eggs and sugar are added to a basic bread dough of flour, yeast, salt and milk. It gives the doughnut a richer, sweeter flavour and a soft, fine texture. I use strong bread flour for the dough because it gives the lightest, softest, most delicious doughnut. However, you can use a combination of plain flour and strong, and even just plain flour — your doughnuts won't be as light, but will still taste good.

I also use fast-action yeast for convenience because it can be added straight to the flour and other dry ingredients without the need to activate it in water first. You can buy it in small containers or sachets from most supermarkets.

For a less rich dough, you can simply mix together flour, yeast, salt and water. It will make a plain bread dough that's virtually fat-free, which you can then decorate as you please.

For a plain doughnut dough mix:
500G/1LB 2OZ PLAIN FLOUR
1 TEASPOON SALT
1 X 7G SACHET FAST-ACTION YEAST
1 TABLESPOON CASTER SUGAR
300-350ML LUKEWARM WATER

MAKING DOUGHNUTS

There are a couple of steps in the dough-making process that are essential.
Once you have combined all of your ingredients you will have to 'knead' them.
Get ready, resume a serious pose. Feet apart. Sleeves rolled up ...

KNEADING

Tip the dough out of your mixing bowl onto a lightly floured surface. Push
the heel of one hand into the dough, slide the dough away from you along the
surface, then bring your hand and dough back to the starting point with your
fingers. Swap hands and repeat the process, you will notice an 'X' on your work
surface. Do this for at least 10 minutes or until you have a beautifully smooth,
soft (but not sticky) elastic dough. This is the method I was taught at cookery
school and I can confirm that it works a treat on both the dough and your upper
arms. The important thing with kneading is to really develop that gluten.

PROVING

The next stage is proving. This allows the dough to rest and for the yeast to do
its thing, developing that lovely doughnut flavour. Pop your dough in a lightly
oiled bowl, cover with a clean cloth and allow it to double in size – this will
normally take about an hour, depending on how warm your kitchen is. To
check if your dough is proved, prod it with your fingertip; if the dent made
stays put you are ready to go. The dough will look smooth and rounded on the
surface and you will have to resist the urge to run your palm over it. Over-
proved dough will look like it is collapsing and may taste yeasty.

KNOCKING BACK

Now your dough is proved you have to 'knock it back' or remove all of the air
produced during the proving stage. To do this, tip the dough out onto a lightly
floured surface and knead as described earlier for a few minutes.

SHAPING

You're now ready to shape your doughnuts: divide the dough into equal parts
using a sharp knife. Take a piece of dough and use your thumb and index finger
to fold the edges of the dough into the centre, creating a round shape. Pinch
the folded edges together and give them a gentle twist, flip over so that the

smooth side is uppermost. Cup your hand over the surface and roll around your palm to shape into a perfect ball. Transfer, smooth side up, to a lined baking sheet.

Your dough balls will need to prove a second time, this usually takes about 30 minutes. To check if they are sufficiently proved, use your fingertip to gently prod the ball near its base. If the dent remains you are ready for cooking.

COOKING

You can fry or bake your doughnut. If you are baking, get to know your oven, identify any hot spots or cold spots. When bread is cooked it should be risen, golden and sound hollow when tapped on the base. If you are going to fry your doughnuts, I would strongly recommend you buy a sugar thermometer to ensure that your can regulate the temperature of the oil. Always lower your doughnuts into hot oil with care using a slotted metal spoon and never leave a pan of hot oil unattended.

FILLING

You should now have beautifully cooked doughnuts ready to be filled. I like to use a piping bag fitted with a nozzle to keep things clean. You could also use a strong sandwich bag with the corner snipped off. If your inner domestic god/ goddess is having a break and filling doughnuts is not floating your boat, decant the fillings into a bowl and take it to the table with the pile of fresh doughnuts. Let everyone dig in, smearing, spreading and enjoying however they see fit!

EATING

Last but not least. All doughnuts are best eaten on the day they are made. If not eaten straightaway, pack the cold doughnuts in an airtight container for the fun to be resumed later.

COOK,S NOTES

You should use unsalted butter and semi-skimmed milk unless I have specified otherwise. The recipes have been tested using medium eggs. Uncooked or partially cooked eggs should not be eaten by the very young, very old, pregnant or immunocompromised people. If doughnuts are filled with fresh cream, soft cheese or custard, ensure they are chilled in a refrigerator until ready to serve. All spoon measures are level, unless otherwise specified.

CHAPTER 1

BAKED

THE CLASSIC

Bake it or fry it, this sugar-coated and jam-filled doughnut stands the test of time. Don't knock it until you've tried it homemade and freshly cooked.

MAKES 12 ——————————————————————————————————

225ML/8FL OZ MILK
50G/2OZ BUTTER, DICED
2 EGGS, LIGHTLY BEATEN
500G/1LB 2OZ STRONG WHITE BREAD
 FLOUR, PLUS EXTRA FOR DUSTING
50G/2OZ CASTER SUGAR
1 X 7G SACHET DRIED FAST-ACTION
 YEAST

To finish
50G/2OZ BUTTER, MELTED (FOR
 BAKED ONLY)
1 LITRE/1¾ PINTS SUNFLOWER
 OIL (FOR FRIED ONLY)
100G/4OZ CASTER SUGAR
175G/6OZ YOUR FAVOURITE JAM

Heat the milk to just below boiling point. Remove from the heat, add the butter and swirl the pan to melt it. Leave to cool for about 5 minutes until you can comfortably dip your little finger into the liquid, then stir in the lightly beaten eggs.

Put the flour, sugar and yeast into a large mixing bowl and stir to combine, then add a pinch of salt. Make a well in the centre of the flour and gradually pour in the milk mixture, stirring, to form a soft, slightly sticky dough.

Tip the dough onto a lightly floured work surface and knead for 10 minutes, or until you have a soft, shiny dough. Place the dough into a lightly

greased bowl, cover with a clean cloth and leave to stand in a warm spot until doubled in size – about 1 hour.

Tip the dough out onto a floured work surface and knead briefly to get rid of any air bubbles. Flatten the dough to a 2cm (1in) thickness. Use a 7cm (3in) round cutter to stamp out the dough or cut into 12 equal parts with a knife, then shape into neat balls. Transfer to two baking trays lined with baking paper, leaving a 5cm (2in) space between each ball. Loosely cover with a cloth, leave to stand for about 30 minutes, or until doubled in size.

Preheat the oven to 180C/350F/ gas 4. Bake the doughnuts for about 12–15 minutes, or until the doughnuts are golden and sound hollow when you tap their underside. Transfer to a wire rack to cool.

To fry, pour the oil into a medium-sized deep saucepan – the oil should be about 5cm (2in) deep – and heat to 160C/325F. Carefully lower 2–3 dough balls at a time into the hot oil and fry for 8 minutes, flipping halfway through, until they are a deep golden brown. Remove with a slotted spoon and drain on kitchen paper. Continue frying until all of the doughnuts are cooked.

To finish, roll the warm fried doughnuts in the caster sugar. For baked doughnuts, brush the warm doughnuts with the melted butter and roll in the sugar.

Once cool enough to handle, use the end of a dessertspoon to make a hole in one side of each doughnut. Wiggle the handle around to create a space for the jam. Spoon the jam into a piping bag fitted with a 0.5mm round nozzle. Squeeze jam into the doughnuts, until you can squeeze no more!

LEMON MERINGUE

Tangy lemon curd and sweet, pillowy meringue are the perfect match.

MAKES 12 ————————————————————————————

225ML/8FL OZ MILK
50G/2OZ BUTTER, DICED
2 EGGS, LIGHTLY BEATEN
500G/1LB 2OZ STRONG WHITE BREAD
  FLOUR, PLUS EXTRA FOR DUSTING
50G/2OZ CASTER SUGAR
1 X 7G SACHET DRIED FAST-ACTION
  YEAST
ZEST 2 LEMONS

For the filling
200G/7OZ LEMON CURD

For the topping
2 EGG WHITES
100G/4OZ CASTER SUGAR

Make up the dough following the method on page 16 (The Classic) to the end of step 4, adding the lemon zest to the other dry ingredients in step 2.

Preheat the oven to 180C/350F/gas 4. Bake the doughnuts for about 12–15 minutes, or until the doughnuts are golden and sound hollow when you tap their underside. Transfer to a wire rack to cool.

Once cool, use the end of a dessertspoon to make a hole in one side of each doughnut. Wiggle the handle around inside to create a little space for the lemon curd. Spoon the curd into a piping bag fitted with a 0.5mm round nozzle. Squeeze the curd into the doughnuts, until you can squeeze no more! Put the doughnuts back on the wire rack.

Whisk the egg whites to stiff peaks, gradually adding the sugar and whisking after each addition until the whites are firm and glossy. Dollop a tablespoon of meringue mix onto each doughnut then flash them under a hot grill or use a blow torch (very exciting) to brown the tops. Enjoy!

RHUBARB & CUSTARD

Two flavours usually reserved for a crumble, but also perfect for a doughnut.

225ML/8FL OZ MILK
50G/2OZ BUTTER, DICED
2 EGGS, LIGHTLY BEATEN
500G/1LB 2OZ STRONG WHITE BREAD
 FLOUR, PLUS EXTRA FOR DUSTING
50G/2OZ CASTER SUGAR
1 X 7G SACHET DRIED FAST-ACTION
 YEAST

For the filling
250G/9OZ RHUBARB, CUT INTO 2CM/1IN
 PIECES

2CM/1IN PIECE FRESH GINGER, GRATED
ZEST 1 ORANGE
50G/2OZ CASTER SUGAR
75ML/2½FL OZ DOUBLE CREAM
½ VANILLA POD, SEEDS SCRAPED
150G POT READY-MADE CUSTARD

To finish
50G/2OZ BUTTER, MELTED
100G/4OZ CASTER SUGAR

Make up the dough following the method on page 16 (The Classic) to the end of step 4.

Put the rhubarb, ginger, orange zest and sugar into a small pan over a low heat. Stir the mixture until the fruit becomes juicy and the sugar completely dissolves. Increase the heat slightly and cook for 8 minutes, or until the rhubarb has broken down and the sauce has thickened. Leave to cool.

For the custard, pour the cream into a mixing bowl with the vanilla seeds and whip to stiff peaks, then gently fold through the custard. Cover and chill.

Preheat the oven to 180C/350F/ gas 4. Bake the doughnuts for about 12–15 minutes, or until the doughnuts are golden and sound hollow when you tap their underside. Transfer to a wire rack to cool. Once cool enough to handle, brush the doughnuts all over with the melted butter then roll them in the sugar. Put them back on the wire rack until cold.

Split the cold doughnuts through the centre and add a dollop of the custard and a generous dollop of rhubarb mixture, then sandwich the two halves together. Enjoy.

ENGLISH PLOUGHMAN'S

A traditional lunch combo, turned into a doughnut!

225ML/8FL OZ MILK
50G/2OZ BUTTER, DICED
2 EGGS, LIGHTLY BEATEN
500G/1LB 2OZ STRONG WHITE BREAD
 FLOUR, PLUS EXTRA FOR DUSTING
50G/2OZ CASTER SUGAR
1 X 7G SACHET DRIED FAST-ACTION
 YEAST

To finish
100G/4OZ MATURE CHEDDAR,
 COARSELY GRATED
4 TBSP SANDWICH PICKLE
50G/2OZ CASTER SUGAR

Make up the dough following the method on page 16 (The Classic) to the end of step 3.

Remove the dough from the bowl and knead briefly on a floured work surface to get rid of any air bubbles. Add three-quarters of the grated cheese in 2 additions, kneading as you do so until the cheese is incorporated into the dough.

Flatten the dough to a 2cm (1in) thickness. Use a 7cm (3in) round cutter to stamp out the dough or cut into 12 equal parts with a knife, then shape each piece of dough into 15cm (6in) long sausage shapes.

Transfer to two baking trays lined with baking paper, leaving a 5cm (2in) space between each length of dough. Spread the top of each doughnut with a teaspoon of pickle then scatter the doughnuts with the remaining cheese. Loosely cover with a cloth and leave to stand for about 30 minutes, or until doubled in size.

Preheat the oven to 180C/350F/ gas 4. Bake the doughnuts for about 18–20 minutes, or until the doughnuts are golden and sound hollow when you tap their underside. Transfer to a wire rack to cool.

CHINESE **PORK**

No more last-minute dashes to Chinatown for a pork bun.

225ML/8FL OZ MILK
50G/2OZ BUTTER, DICED
2 EGGS, LIGHTLY BEATEN
500G/1LB 2OZ STRONG WHITE BREAD
  FLOUR, PLUS EXTRA FOR DUSTING
50G/2OZ CASTER SUGAR
1 X 7G SACHET DRIED FAST-ACTION
  YEAST

For the filling
350G/12OZ PORK LOIN
200ML JAR HOISIN SAUCE
¼ TSP CHINESE FIVE SPICE
1 TBSP DARK SOY SAUCE

For the topping
1 EGG, LIGHTLY BEATEN
1 TSP SESAME SEEDS

Preheat the oven to 190C/375F/gas 5. To make the filling, put the pork loin in a baking dish and spoon over half the hoisin sauce, Chinese five spice and soy sauce. Turn the pork to coat in the sauce then cook for 40 minutes, basting halfway through. Remove from the oven, allow to cool for 15 minutes then chop into 1cm (½in) cubes. Stir through the remaining hoisin sauce.

Make up the dough following the method on page 16 (The Classic) to the end of step 3. Remove the dough from the bowl and knead briefly to get rid of any air bubbles. Flatten the dough to a 1cm (½in) thickness, then roll out to a 30cm x 30cm (12in x 12in) square. Using a knife, cut the dough into 12 equal parts then press

each piece out to a rough 10cm x 10cm (4in x 4in) square. Put 1 heaped tablespoon of pork mixture into the centre of each square. Bring opposite corners of the dough squares together to form a parcel and pinch to seal. Transfer to two baking sheets lined with baking paper, leaving a 5cm (2in) space between each parcel. Loosely cover with a cloth and leave to stand for about 10 minutes.

Preheat the oven to 180C/350F/gas 4. Brush the doughnuts with beaten egg then sprinkle with sesame seeds. Cook for 12–15 minutes, or until the doughnuts are golden and sound hollow when you tap their underside. Transfer to a wire rack to cool slighlty. Enjoy warm.

PIZZA TRIANGLES

I've kept the toppings traditional, but feel free to go mad with your own favourites!

MAKES 8

225ML/8FL OZ MILK
50G/2OZ BUTTER, DICED
2 EGGS, LIGHTLY BEATEN
500G/1LB 2OZ STRONG WHITE BREAD
 FLOUR, PLUS EXTRA FOR DUSTING
50G/2OZ CASTER SUGAR
1 X 7G SACHET DRIED FAST-ACTION
 YEAST

To finish
50G/2OZ RED PESTO
HANDFUL MIXED OLIVES, PITTED
 AND TORN
50G/2OZ GRATED MOZZARELLA
HANDFUL FRESH BASIL
OLIVE OIL FOR DRIZZLING

Make up the dough following the method on page 16 (The Classic) to the end of step 3.

Remove the dough from the bowl and knead briefly on a well-floured work surface to get rid of any air bubbles. Flatten the dough to a 2cm (1in) thick circle with a diameter of 20–25cm (8–10in). Cut the dough into 8 equal segments then pull them apart and transfer the triangles to two baking trays lined with baking paper. Leave a 5cm (2in) space between each pizza triangle.

Spread a generous teaspoon of pesto over the top of each triangle, add a couple of olives then sprinkle with mozzarella. Loosely cover with cling film and leave to stand for about 30 minutes.

Preheat the oven to 180C/350F/ gas 4. Bake the doughnuts for about 12–15 minutes, or until the doughnuts are golden and sound hollow when you tap their underside. Transfer to a wire rack to cool.

Serve scattered with fresh basil and a drizzle of olive oil.

HAZELNUT BOMBOLONI

You can imagine my excitement during a recent trip to Italy when presented with a hazelnut-and-chocolate filled doughnut for BREAKFAST!

MAKES 12 ————————————————————————————————

225ML/8FL OZ MILK
50G/2OZ BUTTER, DICED
2 EGGS, LIGHTLY BEATEN
500G/1LB 2OZ STRONG WHITE BREAD
  FLOUR, PLUS EXTRA FOR DUSTING
50G/2OZ CASTER SUGAR
1 X 7G SACHET DRIED FAST-ACTION
  YEAST
50G/2OZ HAZELNUTS, VERY FINELY
  CHOPPED

For the filling
300G JAR NUTELLA OR YOUR
  FAVOURITE CHOCOLATE HAZELNUT
  SPREAD

To coat
100G/4OZ CASTER SUGAR
50G/2OZ HAZELNUTS, ROUGHLY
  CHOPPED
50G/2OZ BUTTER, MELTED

Make up the dough following the method on page 16 (The Classic) to the end of step 4. Add the finely chopped hazelnuts to the other dry ingredients in step 2.

Preheat the oven to 180C/350F/gas 4. Bake the doughnuts for about 12–15 minutes, or until the doughnuts are golden and sound hollow when you tap their underside. Transfer to a wire rack to cool.

Once cool enough to handle, use the end of a dessertspoon to make a hole in the top of each doughnut. Wiggle the handle around to create space for the filling. Put the caster sugar and half of the roughly chopped hazelnuts into

the bowl of a food processor and whizz until the nuts are finely chopped and combined with the sugar. Brush the doughnuts all over with melted butter then roll in the nutty sugar. Put the doughnuts back on the wire rack and allow to cool.

Spoon the Nutella into a piping bag fitted with a 0.5mm round nozzle. Squeeze the chocolate spread into the doughnuts, until you can squeeze no more – it may start to leak out of the top. Drizzle over any excess then sprinkle with the remaining roughly chopped hazelnuts. Best eaten in the company of friends who are honest enough to tell you if you have chocolate spread all over your face!

FRANKFURTER

The totally transportable, hand-held meal.

225ML/8FL OZ MILK
50G/2OZ BUTTER, DICED
2 EGGS, LIGHTLY BEATEN
500G/1LB 2OZ STRONG WHITE BREAD
FLOUR, PLUS EXTRA FOR DUSTING
50G/2OZ CASTER SUGAR
1 X 7G SACHET DRIED FAST-ACTION
 YEAST

For the filling
4 TSP DIJON MUSTARD
8 FRANKFURTER SAUSAGES

To finish
1 EGG, LIGHTLY BEATEN TO GLAZE

Make up the dough following the method on page 16 (The Classic) to the end of step 3.

Remove the dough from the bowl and knead briefly on a well-floured work surface to get rid of any air bubbles. Flatten the dough to a 1cm (½in) thickness. Cut the dough into 8 equal parts, then press each piece into a 10cm x 15cm (4in x 6in) rectangle.

Spread half a teaspoon of mustard over each square then lay a sausage along the centre of the dough. Fold both sides up and the edges over each other to enclose the frankfurter. Transfer to two baking trays lined with baking paper, placing the dough seam side down. Leave a 5cm (2in) space between each doughnut. Loosely cover with a cloth and leave to stand for about 30 minutes.

To bake, preheat the oven to 180C/350F/gas 4. Brush the doughnuts with a little beaten egg then bake for 15–18 minutes, or until the doughnuts are golden and sound hollow when you tap their underside. Transfer to a wire rack to cool. Serve with extra mustard and sauerkraut, if you like.

BANANA SPLIT

Easy to prepare and no fancy ingredients involved, but what a feast!

MAKES 12 —————————————————————————————

225ML/8FL OZ MILK
50G/2OZ BUTTER, DICED
2 EGGS, LIGHTLY BEATEN
500G/1LB 2OZ STRONG WHITE BREAD
 FLOUR, PLUS EXTRA FOR DUSTING
50G/2OZ CASTER SUGAR
1 X 7G SACHET DRIED FAST-ACTION
 YEAST

For the filling
600ML/1 PINT DOUBLE CREAM
1 TSP VANILLA ESSENCE
2 TBSP CASTER SUGAR
3 BANANAS, THINLY SLICED
2 CHOCOLATE FLAKE BARS, CRUMBLED

Make up the dough following the method on page 16 (The Classic) to the end of step 3.

Remove the dough from the bowl and knead briefly to get rid of any air bubbles. Flatten the dough to a 2cm (1in) thickness. Use a 7cm (3in) round cutter to stamp out the dough or cut into 12 equal parts with a knife, then shape each piece of dough into 15cm (6in) long sausage shapes. Transfer to two baking trays lined with baking paper, leaving a 5cm (2in) space between each length of dough. Loosely cover with a cloth, leave to stand for about 30 minutes, or until doubled in size.

To bake, preheat the oven to 180C/350F/gas 4. Bake the doughnuts for about 12–15 minutes, or until the doughnuts are golden and sound hollow when you tap their underside. Transfer to a wire rack to cool.

To make the filling, whip the cream, vanilla essence and caster sugar to soft peaks. Split the doughnuts lengthways through the top, being careful not to cut through to the base. Gently prise the sides apart, spoon in the cream and poke in slices of banana. Scatter generously with chocolate flakes. (You could serve with ice cream for extra sundae joy.)

MARGARITA RINGS

Like a margarita sipped in the Mexican sun – only these are warm and doughy.

MAKES 12 ————————————————————————————

225ML/8FL OZ MILK
50G/2OZ BUTTER, DICED
2 EGGS, LIGHTLY BEATEN
500G/1LB 2OZ STRONG WHITE BREAD
 FLOUR, PLUS EXTRA FOR DUSTING
50G/2OZ CASTER SUGAR
1 X 7G SACHET DRIED FAST-ACTION
 YEAST
ZEST 2 LIMES
2 RED CHILLIES, FINELY CHOPPED

For the topping
200G/9OZ ICING SUGAR
4–6 TABLESPOONS TEQUILA
SQUEEZE LIME JUICE

To finish
1 TSP DRIED CHILLI FLAKES
½ TSP SEA SALT

Make up the dough following the method on page 16 (The Classic) to the end of step 4, adding the lime zest and chillies to the rest of the dry ingredients in step 2.

Before leaving the shaped balls to double in size, plunge the handle of a wooden spoon into flour, then push it into the centre of each doughnut, going all the way through to the other side. Flip the doughnut, one at a time, onto the handle and rotate the spoon until the hole is about 6cm (2in) wide. Then, transfer to two baking trays lined with baking paper, leaving a 5cm (2in) space between each ring. Loosely cover with a cloth, leave to stand for about 30 minutes, or until doubled in size.

Preheat the oven to 180C/350F/ gas 4. Bake the doughnuts for about 12–15 minutes, or until the doughnuts are golden and sound hollow when you tap their underside. Transfer to a wire rack to cool.

For the topping, mix the icing sugar with the tequila and a squeeze of lime juice to give a thick but runny glaze. Drizzle each doughnut ring with icing and sprinkle with chilli flakes while the glaze is still wet. Allow to cool and sprinkle with a little salt before eating.

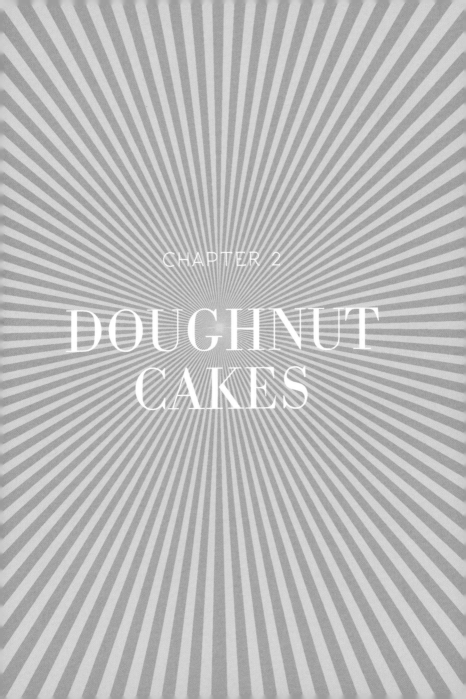

CHAPTER 2

DOUGHNUT CAKES

MARSH**MALLOW**

Not dissimilar to a teacake, but with chocolate cake instead of biscuit.

MAKES 6 LARGE OR 30 MINI (SEE PAGE 88)

100G/4OZ PLAIN FLOUR
1 TSP BAKING POWDER
2 TBSP COCOA POWDER
75G/2½OZ DARK SOFT BROWN SUGAR
1 EGG, LIGHTLY BEATEN
2 TBSP SUNFLOWER OIL, PLUS EXTRA
  FOR GREASING
100G/4OZ FAT-FREE NATURAL YOGURT

For the filling
100G/4OZ MINI MARSHMALLOWS

For the topping
100G/4OZ PLAIN CHOCOLATE (70%
  COCOA SOLIDS)
1 TBSP DESICCATED COCONUT

Preheat the oven to 180C/350F/ gas 4. Put the flour, baking powder, cocoa, sugar, egg, oil and yogurt into a mixing bowl and beat until smooth.

Use 2 teaspoons to dollop the mixture into a greased doughnut tin, making sure you don't cover the middle with mixture.

Bake for 10–12 minutes, or until risen and springy to the touch. Leave to cool in the tin for a few minutes, then transfer the doughnuts to a wire rack to cool completely.

Put the mini marshmallows and 2 tablespoons boiling water into a heatproof mixing bowl set over a pan of barely simmering water, and stir continuously with a wooden spoon until the marshmallows melt and become thick and shiny.

Split each doughnut ring through the centre and spoon the marshmallow equally over the bases, sandwich with the doughnut tops and put back onto the wire rack.

Put the chocolate into a small microwaveable bowl and heat in 20-second intervals, stirring after each one until the chocolate is silky smooth. Slide a baking tray under the wire rack to catch any drips then drizzle the chocolate over the doughnuts and decorate with the coconut. Allow the chocolate to set before serving.

CHERRY BAKEWELL

All the taste and texture of a Bakewell tart but without the calorie-packed pastry. Makes you feel quite smug really – providing you don't eat them all!

MAKES 6

85G/3OZ PLAIN FLOUR
1 TSP BAKING POWDER
50G/2OZ GROUND ALMONDS
75G/2½OZ CASTER SUGAR
1 EGG, LIGHTLY BEATEN
2 TBSP SUNFLOWER OIL, PLUS EXTRA
  FOR GREASING
100G/4OZ FAT-FREE NATURAL YOGURT

½ TSP ALMOND ESSENCE
25G/1OZ GLACÉ CHERRIES, FINELY
  CHOPPED

For the topping
140G/5OZ ICING SUGAR
1 TBSP TOASTED FLAKED ALMONDS

Preheat the oven to 180C/350F/ gas 4. Put the flour, baking powder, ground almonds, sugar, egg, oil, yogurt and almond essence into a mixing bowl and beat until smooth. Gently fold through the cherries.

Use 2 teaspoons to dollop the mixture into a greased doughnut tin, making sure you don't cover the middle with mixture.

Bake for 10–12 minutes, or until risen and springy to the touch. Leave to cool in the tin for a few minutes, then transfer the doughnuts to a wire rack to cool completely.

To make the topping, mix the icing sugar with 1–1½ tablespoons of water to get a thick, smooth icing that you can drizzle. Slide a baking tray under the wire rack to catch any drips then spoon the icing over the doughnuts. Scatter the almonds over the tops and allow to set before eating.

COCONUT & LIME

These lovely, zingy doughnuts will lift your spirits and may even make you break out into a little dance.

MAKES 6 LARGE OR 30 MINI (SEE PAGE 88)

100G/4OZ PLAIN FLOUR
1 TSP BAKING POWDER
75G/2½OZ CASTER SUGAR
3 TBSP DESICCATED COCONUT
1 EGG, LIGHTLY BEATEN
2 TBSP SUNFLOWER OIL, PLUS EXTRA
  FOR GREASING

100G/4OZ FAT-FREE NATURAL YOGURT
ZEST 2 LIMES

For the drizzle
JUICE 2 LIMES
50G/2OZ CASTER SUGAR

Preheat the oven to 180C/350F/ gas 4. Put the flour, baking powder, sugar, desiccated coconut, egg, oil, yogurt and zest of 1 lime into a mixing bowl and beat until smooth.

Use 2 teaspoons to dollop the mixture into a greased doughnut tin, making sure you don't cover the middle with mixture.

Bake for 10–12 minutes, or until risen, springy to the touch and a light golden colour. Leave to cool in the tin for a few minutes, then use a toothpick or tip of a sharp knife to prick the doughnuts all over.

To make the drizzle, mix the remaining lime zest with the juice and caster sugar, then spoon a little over the doughnuts allowing it to sink in. Continue spooning over the syrup as the doughnuts cool. Allow to cool completely in the tin. Carefully remove and eat with a fork!

VERY BERRY

Fresh berries are to be found here, there and everywhere in these sophisticated doughnuts. Perfect for afternoon tea.

MAKES 6

85G/3OZ PLAIN FLOUR
1 TSP BAKING POWDER
50G/2OZ GROUND ALMONDS
2 TSP FREEZE-DRIED RASPBERRIES OR STRAWBERRIES
75G/2½OZ CASTER SUGAR
1 EGG, LIGHTLY BEATEN
2 TBSP SUNFLOWER OIL, PLUS EXTRA FOR GREASING
75G/2½OZ FAT-FREE NATURAL YOGURT

50G/2OZ RASPBERRIES, MASHED WITH A FORK
18 SMALL BLUEBERRIES, PLUS EXTRA TO SERVE

For the topping
100G/4OZ RASPBERRIES, MASHED WITH A FORK
85G/3OZ GRANULATED SUGAR

Preheat the oven to 180C/350F/ gas 4. Put the flour, baking powder, ground almonds, freeze-dried berries and sugar into a bowl. In another bowl mix the egg, oil, yogurt and mashed raspberries together then stir into the dry ingredients and beat until smooth.

Use 2 teaspoons to dollop the mixture into a greased doughnut tin, making sure you don't cover the middle with mixture. Dot 3 blueberries into each of the doughnuts, pushing lightly to submerge the berries just under the surface of the batter.

Bake for 10–12 minutes, or until risen and springy to the touch. Leave to cool in the tin for a few minutes, then transfer to a wire rack to cool.

To make the topping, set a fine meshed sieve over a mixing bowl then push the mashed raspberries through. Discard the seeds. Stir the sugar into the raspberry juice then drizzle over the doughnuts. Allow the sugar to set then serve with extra berries, if you like.

PISTACHIO & ORANGE BLOSSOM

Adorned with pistachios and laced with orange blossom, these elegant, green goodies are really quite exotic.

MAKES 6 LARGE OR 30 MINI (SEE PAGE 88) ————————————————

50G/2OZ SHELLED PISTACHIO NUTS
75G/2½OZ CASTER SUGAR
85G/3OZ PLAIN FLOUR
2 TBSP SUNFLOWER OIL, PLUS EXTRA
 FOR GREASING
1 EGG, LIGHTLY BEATEN
100G/4OZ FAT-FREE NATURAL YOGURT
1 TSP ORANGE BLOSSOM WATER

For the topping
140G/5OZ ICING SUGAR
½ TSP ORANGE BLOSSOM WATER
FEW DROPS GREEN FOOD COLOURING
1 TBSP SHELLED PISTACHIO NUTS,
 FINELY CHOPPED

Preheat the oven to 180C/350F/ gas 4. Put the pistachios and caster sugar into the bowl of a food processor and whizz until the pistachios are very finely chopped – almost to a powder. Tip the nuts and sugar into a mixing bowl and add the flour, oil, egg, yogurt and orange blossom water and beat until smooth.

Use 2 teaspoons to dollop the mixture into a greased doughnut tin, making sure you don't cover the middles with mixture.

Bake for 10–12 minutes, or until risen and springy to the touch. Leave to cool in the tin for a few minutes, then transfer the doughnuts to a wire rack to cool completely.

To make the topping, mix the icing sugar, orange blossom water and a few drops of food colouring with 1–1½ tablespoons of water to give a smooth, slightly runny consistency. Slide a tray under the wire rack to catch any drips then drizzle each of the doughnuts with the glaze, sprinkle with the chopped pistachios and transfer to the wire rack to set.

PEACHES & CREAM

The perfect way to showcase ripe juicy peaches in summer.

MAKES 6

100G/4OZ PLAIN FLOUR
1 TSP BAKING POWDER
75G/2½OZ LIGHT SOFT BROWN SUGAR
1 EGG, LIGHTLY BEATEN
2 TBSP SUNFLOWER OIL, PLUS EXTRA
  FOR GREASING
100G/4OZ PEACH YOGURT

For the filling
300ML/11FL OZ DOUBLE CREAM
2 TBSP PEACH LIQUEUR
1 TBSP ICING SUGAR
3 RIPE PEACHES, HALVED, STONED AND
  THINLY SLICED

For the topping
ICING SUGAR, FOR DUSTING

Preheat the oven to 180C/350F/ gas 4. Put the flour, baking powder, sugar, egg, oil and yogurt into a mixing bowl and beat until smooth.

Use 2 teaspoons to dollop the mixture into a greased doughnut tin, making sure you don't cover the middles with mixture.

Bake for 10–12 minutes, or until risen and springy to the touch. Leave to cool in the tin for a few minutes, then transfer the doughnuts to a wire rack to cool completely.

Lightly whip the cream with the peach liqueur and icing sugar until it just holds its shape. Split each cooled doughnut ring through the centre. Divide the cream between the bases, lay peach slices on top then sandwich them with the doughnut tops. Dust each with a little icing sugar before serving.

JAFFA CAKE

Zesty sponge covered in rich, dark chocolate, the addition of jelly bringing back happy memories of a childhood favourite. (Okay, an adult favourite too!)

MAKES 6 LARGE OR 30 MINI (SEE PAGE 88)

100G/4OZ PLAIN FLOUR
1 TSP BAKING POWDER
75G/2½OZ SOFT LIGHT BROWN SUGAR
1 EGG, LIGHTLY BEATEN
2 TBSP SUNFLOWER OIL, PLUS EXTRA
 FOR GREASING
100G/4OZ FAT-FREE NATURAL YOGURT
ZEST 1 ORANGE

For the topping
85G/3OZ PLAIN CHOCOLATE FLAVOURED
 WITH ORANGE (70% COCOA SQLIDS)
½ X 135G PACK ORANGE-FLAVOURED
 JELLY
3 TBSP ORANGE JUICE
ZEST 1 ORANGE, TO DECORATE

Preheat the oven to 180C/350F/ gas 4. Put the flour, baking powder, sugar, egg, oil, yogurt and orange zest into a mixing bowl and beat until smooth.

Use 2 teaspoons to dollop the mixture into a greased doughnut tin, making sure you don't cover the middle with mixture.

Bake for 10–12 minutes, or until risen and springy to the touch. Leave to cool in the tin for a few minutes, then transfer the doughnuts to a wire rack to cool completely.

Set a large heatproof bowl over a pan of barely simmering water, add the chocolate, jelly and orange juice and stir until the chocolate has melted and the topping is smooth.

Slide a baking tray under the wire rack to catch any drips then spoon the topping over the doughnuts. Sprinkle with orange zest while the topping is still wet, then allow to set before eating.

RUM & RAISIN

These little fellas look so innocent, but underneath their angelic exterior, juicy rummy raisins are just waiting to be devoured.

75G/2½OZ RAISINS
2 TBSP DARK RUM
100G/4OZ PLAIN FLOUR
1 TSP BAKING POWDER
75G/2½OZ SOFT DARK BROWN SUGAR
1 EGG, LIGHTLY BEATEN
2 TBSP SUNFLOWER OIL, PLUS EXTRA
 FOR GREASING
85G/3OZ FAT-FREE NATURAL YOGURT

For the topping
100G/4OZ ICING SUGAR
1–2 TBSP DARK RUM

Preheat the oven to 180C/350F/gas 4. Put the raisins and rum into a bowl and allow to stand for 15 minutes. Add the flour, baking powder, sugar, egg, oil and yogurt and beat until smooth.

Use 2 teaspoons to dollop the mixture into a greased doughnut tin, making sure you don't cover the middle with mixture.

Bake for 10–12 minutes, or until risen and springy to the touch. Leave to cool in the tin for a few minutes, then transfer the doughnuts to a wire rack to cool completely.

To make the topping, mix the icing sugar with enough rum to give a smooth, slightly runny consistency. Slide a baking tray under the wire rack then dip each of the doughnuts into the glaze and allow to set before serving.

BOOZY CHOCOLATE CHERRY

Booze (yes please), chocolate (never say no) and cherries (one of my five a day?).

MAKES 6 LARGE OR 30 MINI (SEE PAGE 88) ————————————————

100G/4OZ PLAIN FLOUR
1 TSP BAKING POWDER
2 TBSP COCOA POWDER
75G/2½OZ DARK SOFT BROWN SUGAR
1 EGG, LIGHTLY BEATEN
2 TBSP SUNFLOWER OIL, PLUS EXTRA
  FOR GREASING
100G/4OZ FAT-FREE NATURAL YOGURT

For the filling
425G CAN CHERRIES IN LIGHT SYRUP,
  DRAINED AND SYRUP RESERVED
2 TBSP BRANDY OR KIRSCH
300ML/11FL OZ DOUBLE CREAM

For the topping
85G/3OZ PLAIN CHOCOLATE (70%
  COCOA SOLIDS)

Preheat the oven to 180C/350F/ gas 4. Put the flour, baking powder, cocoa, sugar, egg, oil and yogurt into a mixing bowl and beat until smooth.

Use 2 teaspoons to dollop the mixture into a greased doughnut tin, making sure you don't cover the middles with mixture.

Bake for 10–12 minutes, or until risen and springy to the touch. Leave to cool in the tin for a few minutes, then transfer the doughnuts to a wire rack to cool completely.

Heat the cherry syrup in a small pan over a medium-high heat until it has reduced by two-thirds. Remove the pan from the heat and allow to cool slightly.

Stir in the brandy or kirsch. Lightly whip the cream until it just holds its shape. Roughly chop about two-thirds of the cherries then gently fold them through the cream.

Split each ring through the centre and spoon over 1–2 teaspoons of the cherry-brandy sauce, allowing it to soak in. Divide the cherry cream between the bases, sandwich with the doughnut tops and spoon over any remaining syrup.

Put the chocolate in a small microwaveable bowl, heat in 20-second intervals, stirring after each one, until silky smooth. Drizzle the melted chocolate over the doughnuts and decorate with the reserved cherries.

PEANUT BUTTER & JAM

I am slightly obsessed with the combination of sweet and savoury; there is something so rightly wrong about it that I cannot stop experimenting! This classic is just right, with no experimentation needed.

MAKES 6 LARGE OR 30 MINI (SEE PAGE 88)

100G/4OZ PLAIN FLOUR
1 TSP BAKING POWDER
75G/2½OZ SOFT LIGHT BROWN SUGAR
1 EGG, LIGHTLY BEATEN
2 TBSP SUNFLOWER OIL, PLUS EXTRA
  FOR GREASING
100G/4OZ FAT-FREE NATURAL YOGURT
2 HEAPED TBSP CRUNCHY PEANUT
  BUTTER

For the filling
6 HEAPED TBSP CRUNCHY PEANUT
  BUTTER
100G/4OZ ICING SUGAR
4 TBSP OF YOUR FAVOURITE JAM

Preheat the oven to 180C/350F/ gas 4. Put the flour, baking powder, sugar, egg, oil, yogurt and peanut butter into a mixing bowl and beat until smooth.

Use 2 teaspoons to dollop the mixture into a greased doughnut tin, making sure you don't cover the middle with mixture.

Bake for 10–12 minutes, or until risen and springy to the touch. Leave to cool in the tin for a few minutes, then transfer the doughnuts to a wire rack to cool completely.

To make the filling, beat the peanut butter and icing sugar with 2–3 tablespoons of hot water, until you have a creamy, spreadable mixture.

Split each ring through the centre, spread the peanut butter filling evenly over the bottom of each of the doughnuts, then spread 2 teaspoons of jam over the top. Sandwich the top and bottom of the doughnuts together.

CHAPTER 3

FRIED

CHURROS & CHOCOLATE SAUCE

Traditional, light, fluffy fried churros with a chilli-spiked chocolate sauce.
These are guaranteed to fire you up.

85G/3OZ BUTTER, DICED
140G/5OZ PLAIN FLOUR, SIFTED
3 EGGS, LIGHTLY BEATEN

For the chocolate sauce
200G/7OZ PLAIN CHOCOLATE (70%
  COCOA SOLIDS), ROUGHLY CHOPPED
150ML/¼ PINT DOUBLE CREAM

2 TBSP GOLDEN SYRUP
¼ TSP CHILLI POWDER
¼ TSP GROUND CINNAMON

To finish
1 LITRE /1¾ PINTS SUNFLOWER OIL
100G/4OZ CASTER SUGAR

Put the butter into a medium-sized pan with 225ml/8fl oz water and heat gently to melt the butter. Once melted, increase the heat and bring to the boil. Remove from the heat and add the flour and beat the mixture until you get a smooth, shiny dough that leaves the sides of the pan. Tip into a mixing bowl and allow to cool for 5 minutes.

Gradually add the eggs and continue to beat until you have a smooth dough. Pile the dough into a piping bag fitted with a 1cm (½in) star-shaped nozzle and allow to rest for 15 minutes.

For the chocolate sauce, put the chocolate into a mixing bowl. Heat the double cream, syrup and spices in a small pan until just below boiling point. Remove from the heat and add to the chocolate. Allow to stand for a few minutes then stir until smooth.

Pour the oil into a medium-sized, deep saucepan – the oil should be about 5cm (2in) deep – and heat the oil to 180C/350F. Quickly dip the end of a pair of kitchen scissors into the hot oil. Hold the piping bag with one hand about 5cm above the surface of the oil. Squeeze out the dough and use the scissors to cut strips at 10cm intervals. Do this in batches, frying for 2–3 minutes, or until golden and puffed up. Remove with a slotted spoon and drain on kitchen paper. Roll the warm churros in the caster sugar and serve with chocolate sauce.

SKANDI CARDAMOM

The traditional Scandinavian flavours of cardamom and cinnamon make these fried doughnuts a simple winner.

MAKES 12 ───────────────────────────────

225ML/8FL OZ MILK
50G/2OZ BUTTER, DICED
2 EGGS, LIGHTLY BEATEN
500G/1LB 2OZ STRONG WHITE BREAD
 FLOUR, PLUS EXTRA FOR DUSTING
50G/2OZ CASTER SUGAR
1 X 7G SACHET DRIED FAST-ACTION
 YEAST

3 CARDAMOM PODS, SEEDS ONLY
BASHED TO A FINE POWDER
½ TSP GROUND CINNAMON

To finish
1 LITRE/1¾ PINTS SUNFLOWER OIL
100G/4OZ CASTER SUGAR
1 TSP GROUND CINNAMON

Make up the dough following the method on page 16 (The Classic) to the end of step 4, adding the ground cardamom and cinnamon to the ingredients at step 2.

Before leaving the shaped balls to double in size, plunge the handle of a wooden spoon into flour, then push it into the centre of each doughnut, going all the way through to the other side. Flip the doughnut onto the handle and rotate until the hole is 6–8cm (2–3in) wide. Continue with the remaining doughnuts.

Transfer to two baking trays lined with baking paper, leaving a 5cm (2in) space between each ring. Loosely cover with a cloth and leave to stand for about 30 minutes, or until doubled in size.

Pour the oil into a medium-sized, deep saucepan – the oil should be about 5cm (2in) deep – and heat the oil to 160C/325F. Carefully lower 2–3 doughnuts at a time into the hot oil and fry for 6 minutes, flipping halfway through, until a deep golden brown. Remove with a slotted spoon and drain on kitchen paper. Continue frying until all of the doughnuts are cooked.

Mix the caster sugar and cinnamon together on a baking tray then roll the warm doughnuts in the mix. Eat warm.

GULAB JAMUN

Although usually scented with rose water, these jamun are made with Chai tea.

MAKES 24

140G/5OZ SKIMMED MILK POWDER
85G/3OZ PLAIN FLOUR
½ TSP BAKING POWDER
¼ TSP BICARBONATE OF SODA
1 CARDAMOM POD, SEEDS ONLY
 BASHED TO A POWDER
250ML/9FL OZ DOUBLE CREAM

For the syrup
200G/7OZ CASTER SUGAR
4 CARDAMOM PODS, BASHED
1 CINNAMON STICK
PINCH SAFFRON STRANDS
1 X SPICED CHAI TEA BAG

To finish
1 LITRE/1¾ PINTS SUNFLOWER OIL

Put the milk powder, flour, baking powder, bicarbonate of soda and cardamom into a large mixing bowl. Stir to combine, then gradually add the cream. Use your hands to work the mixture into a firm, sticky dough.

With slightly damp hands, grab small pieces of dough and roll into 24 walnut-sized balls. Transfer to a baking tray lined with baking paper and chill for 30 minutes.

To make the syrup, put the sugar, cardamom pods, cinnamon and saffron into a large pan with 600ml (1 pint) cold water. Slowly bring to the boil, add the tea bag then simmer for 8 minutes, or until reduced and slightly syrupy. Remove from the heat, take out the tea bag and pour into a deep baking tray. Leave to cool.

Pour the oil into a medium-sized, deep saucepan – the oil should be about 5cm (2in) deep – and heat the oil to 150C/300F. Carefully lower 2–3 doughnuts into the oil. Gently flick the doughnuts after a few seconds to make sure they are not sticking to the base of the pan. Fry for 8 minutes, turning frequently, until a deep golden brown. Remove with a slotted spoon and drain on kitchen paper. Continue frying until all of the doughnuts are cooked. Allow to cool.

Add the doughnuts to the syrup, tilting the tray to coat the balls, then leave to stand for at least 1 hour before eating. The doughnuts will swell up as they absorb the sweet syrup.

OLIBOLLEN

My granddad Arie was a rather surly Dutchman. Once a year he would put aside his grumpy pumps to produce huge piles of these spiced apple and sultana delights.

MAKES 12

175ML/6FL OZ MILK
25G/1OZ BUTTER, DICED
2 EGGS, LIGHTLY BEATEN
300G/11OZ STRONG WHITE BREAD
 FLOUR
75G/2½OZ CASTER SUGAR
1 X 7G SACHET DRIED FAST-ACTION
 YEAST
1 TSP GROUND CINNAMON

¼ NUTMEG, FINELY GRATED
75G/2½OZ SULTANAS
2 SMALL APPLES, CORED AND CUT
 INTO 1CM/½IN DICE

To finish
1 LITRE/1¾ PINTS SUNFLOWER OIL
ICING SUGAR, TO DUST
READY-MADE TOFFEE SAUCE

Heat the milk to just below boiling point. Remove from the heat, add the butter and swirl the pan to melt it. Leave to cool for about 5 minutes until you can comfortably dip your little finger into the liquid, then stir in the lightly beaten eggs.

Put the flour, sugar, yeast, spices, sultanas and apples into a large mixing bowl and stir to combine, then add a pinch of salt. Gradually stir in the milk mixture to form a sticky, wet dough. Cover and leave to stand for 45 minutes.

Pour the oil into a medium-sized, deep saucepan – the oil should be

about 5cm (2in) deep – and heat the oil to 160C/325F. Quickly dip 2 dessertspoons into the hot oil, then scoop heaped spoonfuls of mixture with one of the spoons and use the other to push the mixture into the hot oil). Fry 2–3 olibollen at a time for 8 minutes, flipping halfway through, until they turn a deep golden brown. Remove with a slotted spoon and drain on kitchen paper. Continue frying until all of the doughnuts are cooked.

To finish, dust with icing sugar and drizzle generously with shop-bought toffee sauce. Enjoy warm.

ELDERFLOWER CREAMS

Decorate these elegant, floral bakes with a few silver sugar balls, if you like.

MAKES 12

225ML/8FL OZ MILK
50G/2OZ BUTTER, DICED
2 EGGS, LIGHTLY BEATEN
500G/1LB 2OZ STRONG WHITE BREAD
  FLOUR, PLUS EXTRA FOR DUSTING
50G/2OZ CASTER SUGAR
1 X 7G SACHET DRIED FAST-ACTION
  YEAST

For frying
1 LITRE/1¾ PINTS SUNFLOWER OIL

For the filling
200ML/7FL OZ DOUBLE CREAM
2 TBSP ELDERFLOWER CORDIAL
1 TSP VANILLA EXTRACT
2 TBSP ICING SUGAR

To finish
140G/5OZ ICING SUGAR
2 TBSP ELDERFLOWER CORDIAL
SILVER GLITTER BALLS, TO DECORATE
(OPTIONAL)

Make up the dough following the method on page 16 (The Classic) to the end of step 4.

Pour the oil into a medium-sized, deep saucepan – the oil should be about 5cm (2in) deep – and heat the oil to 160C/325F. Carefully lower 2–3 doughnuts at a time into the hot oil and fry for 8 minutes, flipping halfway through, until a deep golden brown. Remove with a slotted spoon and drain on kitchen paper. Continue frying until all of the doughnuts are cooked. Transfer to a wire rack to cool completely.

Use the end of a dessertspoon to make a hole in one side of each cold doughnut. Wiggle the handle around to create a little cave for the elderflower cream.

To make the filling, whip the cream, elderflower cordial, vanilla and icing sugar to stiff peaks, then spoon into a piping bag fitted with a 0.5mm round nozzle. Squeeze the cream into the doughnuts then return them to the wire rack.

To finish the doughnuts, mix the icing sugar and elderflower cordial until you have a thick, smooth icing.

Use a round-ended knife to spread the icing over the doughnuts. If you are using silver balls to decorate, dot them over while the icing is still wet.

Allow to set for a few minutes before eating, or transfer to the fridge until ready to enjoy.

SALTED CARAMEL

Get involved with these irresistible, sugary, salty caramel doughnuts –
finger-lickingly, lip-lickety good.

MAKES 12

225ML/8FL OZ MILK
50G/2OZ BUTTER, DICED
2 EGGS, LIGHTLY BEATEN
500G/1LB 2OZ STRONG WHITE BREAD
  FLOUR, .PLUS EXTRA FOR DUSTING
50G/2OZ CASTER SUGAR
1 X 7G SACHET DRIED FAST-ACTION
  YEAST

For frying
1 LITRE/1¾ PINTS SUNFLOWER OIL

For the filling
100G/4OZ CASTER SUGAR MIXED WITH
  A PINCH OF SALT
175G/6OZ DULCE DE LECHE OR THICK
  CARAMEL SAUCE
1 TSP SEA SALT

Make up the dough, following the
method on page 16 (The Classic)
to the end of step 4.

Pour the oil into a medium-sized,
deep saucepan – the oil should be
about 5cm (2in) deep – and heat the
oil to 160C/325F. Carefully lower
2–3 dough balls at a time into the
hot oil and fry for 8 minutes, flipping
halfway through, until a deep golden
brown. Remove with a slotted spoon
and drain on kitchen paper. Continue
frying until all of the doughnuts are
cooked.

Roll the warm doughnuts in the salted
caster sugar.

Once they are cool enough to handle,
use the end of a dessertspoon to make
a hole in one side of each doughnut.
Wiggle the handle around to create a
little cave for the caramel filling. Mix
the teaspoon of salt into the caramel
then spoon into a piping bag fitted
with a 0.5mm round nozzle. Squeeze
the caramel into the doughnuts, until
you can squeeze no more!

RICOTTA, ROSEMARY & HONEY

Scented and sweet – a match made in heaven.

MAKES 24

200G/7OZ PLAIN FLOUR
2 TSP BAKING POWDER
1 TBSP FINELY CHOPPED ROSEMARY
3 TBSP RUNNY HONEY
140G/5OZ RICOTTA
3 EGGS, LIGHTLY BEATEN

To finish
1 LITRE/1¾ PINTS SUNFLOWER OIL
RUNNY HONEY, FOR DRIZZLING
(OPTIONAL)

Put the flour, baking powder and rosemary into a mixing bowl and stir to combine.

In another bowl mix the honey, ricotta and eggs. Add the wet ingredients to the dry ingredients until just combined, being careful not to overwork the mixture.

Pour the oil into a medium-sized, deep saucepan – the oil should be about 5cm (2in) deep – and heat the oil to 180C/350F. Quickly dip a couple of teaspoons into the hot oil, then scoop teaspoons of the mixture with one spoon and use the other to slide the mixture off into the hot oil. Fry for 4 minutes, flipping halfway through. Remove with a slotted spoon and drain on kitchen paper. Continue frying until all of the mixture is used up.

Serve warm drizzled with extra honey, if you like.

SPICY CHICKEN

The perfect little portable snack.

MAKES 8

300G/11OZ PLAIN FLOUR, PLUS EXTRA
  FOR DUSTING
3 TSP BAKING POWDER
1 TBSP CASTER SUGAR
1 TBSP SMOKED PAPRIKA
½ TSP HOT CHILLI POWDER
50G/2OZ BUTTER, DICED
175ML/6FL OZ MILK

For the filling
140G/5OZ COOKED CHICKEN (I USED
  HOT AND SPICY), CHOPPED INTO 1CM
  (½IN) CUBES

To finish
1 LITRE/1¾ PINTS SUNFLOWER OIL

Put the plain flour, baking powder, caster sugar and spices into a mixing bowl and stir to combine. Add the diced butter then rub in with your fingertips until the mixture resembles fine breadcrumbs.

Gently heat the milk until just warm. Add to the dry ingredients and use a round-ended knife to form a soft dough. Tip out onto a lightly floured work surface and knead briefly to make a soft dough.

Add a little more flour to the surface then roll the dough out to form a 30cm x 20cm (12in x 8in) rectangle. Divide the rectangle in half horizontally, then make 4 cuts vertically to give 8 equal-sized rectangles.

Place a heaped spoonful of the cooked chicken at one end of the rectangle, leaving a small border around the edge. Run a wet finger around the border, then fold over the dough to enclose the filling. Seal the parcels with a fork. Continue to do this until all of the parcels are made. Chill for 10 minutes.

Pour the oil into a medium-sized, deep saucepan – the oil should be about 5cm (2in) deep – and heat the oil to 160C/325F. Carefully lower 2–3 parcels at a time into the hot oil and fry for 8 minutes, flipping halfway through. Remove with a slotted spoon and drain on kitchen paper. Continue frying until all of the spicy chicken parcels are cooked.

MAPLE BACON

Is it a waffle? Is it a pancake? Is it a doughnut? It's pure pleasure, that's what it is… Rich, maple-flavoured, salty bacon combined with fluffy dough – what more could you wish for?

MAKES 12 ————————————————————————————————————

175ML/6FL OZ MILK

2 EGGS, LIGHTLY BEATEN

4 TBSP MAPLE SYRUP

300G/11OZ STRONG WHITE BREAD
  FLOUR

1 X 7G SACHET DRIED FAST-ACTION
  YEAST

To finish

1 LITRE/1¾ PINTS SUNFLOWER OIL

200G/7OZ ICING SUGAR

4–5 TBSP MAPLE SYRUP

1 X 55G PACKET CRISPY, COOKED
  BACON RASHERS, VERY FINELY
  CHOPPED

Heat the milk to just below boiling point. Remove from the heat and leave to cool for about 5 minutes until you can comfortably dip your little finger into the liquid, then stir in the lightly beaten eggs and the maple syrup.

Put the flour and yeast into large mixing bowl and add a pinch of salt. Gradually stir in the milk mixture to form a sticky wet dough. Cover and leave to stand for 45 minutes.

Pour the oil into a medium-sized, deep saucepan – the oil should be about 5cm (2in) deep – and heat the oil to 160C/325F. Quickly dip 2 dessertspoons into the hot oil, scoop heaped spoonfuls of dough with one

of the spoons then use the other to push the mixture off into the hot oil. Fry 2–3 doughnuts at a time for 8 minutes, flipping halfway through, until a deep golden brown. Remove with a slotted spoon and drain on kitchen paper. Continue frying until all of the doughnuts are cooked. Allow to cool for 10 minutes.

Combine the icing sugar and enough maple syrup to make a thick, spreadable glaze. Put the chopped bacon in a wide shallow bowl. Use a round-ended knife to spread the icing over the top of the doughnuts, then plunge them, icing side down, into the bacon. Allow the topping to set before eating.

TOFFEE & CHOCOLATE

My favourite chocolate bar in the form of a doughnut. It doesn't get much better than this!

225ML/8FL OZ MILK
50G/2OZ BUTTER, DICED, PLUS EXTRA
 FOR GREASING
2 EGGS, LIGHTLY BEATEN
500G/1LB 2OZ STRONG WHITE BREAD
 FLOUR, PLUS EXTRA FOR DUSTING
50G/2OZ CASTER SUGAR
1 X 7G SACHET DRIED FAST-ACTION
 YEAST

For frying
1 LITRE/1¾ PINTS SUNFLOWER OIL

To finish
175G/6OZ DULCE DE LECHE OR THICK
 CARAMEL SAUCE
75G/2½OZ CHOCOLATE-COATED PUFFED
 RICE CEREAL
100G/4OZ MILK CHOCOLATE, MELTED
 AND COOLED

Make up the dough following the method on page 16 (The Classic) to the end of step 3.

Remove the dough from the bowl and knead briefly on a well-floured work surface to get rid of any air bubbles. Flatten the dough to a 2cm (1in) thickness. Use a 7cm (3in) round cutter to stamp out the dough or cut into 12 equal parts with a knife, then shape each piece of dough into 10cm (6in) long sausage shapes.

Transfer to two baking trays lined with baking paper, leaving a 5cm (2in) space between each length of dough.

Loosely cover with a cloth and leave to stand for about 30 minutes, or until doubled in size.

Pour the oil into a medium-sized, deep saucepan – the oil should be about 5cm (2in) deep – and heat the oil to 160C/325F. Carefully lower 2–3 doughnuts at a time into the hot oil and fry for 8 minutes, flipping halfway through, until a deep golden brown. Remove with a slotted spoon and drain on kitchen paper. Continue frying until all of the doughnuts are cooked. Transfer to a wire rack to cool.

Spread the top of the doughnuts with about 1 tablespoon of dulce de leche. Tip the puffed rice cereal into a wide shallow bowl then plunge the doughnuts, toffee side down, into them. Roll the doughnuts from side to side to ensure a good covering of cereal.

Put the doughnuts back on the wire rack, slide a piece of baking paper underneath the rack to catch any drips then spoon a little melted chocolate over each doughnut. Allow the chocolate to set completely before eating these messy treats.

CHAPTER 4

CELEBRATE

ROCKY MOUNTAIN

What started as a road turned into a mountain! The perfect treat for chocoholics.

MAKES 40

225ML/8FL OZ MILK
50G/2OZ BUTTER, DICED
2 EGGS, LIGHTLY BEATEN
500G/1LB 2OZ STRONG WHITE BREAD
  FLOUR, PLUS EXTRA FOR DUSTING
50G/2OZ CASTER SUGAR
1 X 7G SACHET DRIED FAST-ACTION
  YEAST
3 TBSP COCOA POWDER

To build and decorate the tower
2 X 180G BAGS MINI MARSHMALLOWS
200G/7OZ PLAIN CHOCOLATE (70%
  COCOA SOLIDS), MELTED AND COOLED
DECORATIONS OF YOUR CHOICE

Make up the dough following the method on page 16, (The Classic) adding the cocoa powder to the rest of the dry ingredients at step 2.

Remove the dough from the bowl and knead briefly on a well-floured work surface to get rid of any air bubbles. Flatten the dough to a 1cm (½in) thickness. Use a 5cm (2in) round cutter to stamp out the dough or cut into 40 equal parts with a knife, then shape into neat balls.

Transfer to two baking trays lined with baking paper, leaving a 2cm (1in) space between each ball. Loosely cover with a cloth and leave to stand for about 30 minutes, or until doubled in size.

Preheat the oven to 180C/350F/ gas 4. Bake the doughnuts for about 8 minutes, or until the doughnuts are golden and sound hollow when you tap their underside. Transfer to a wire rack to cool.

Put three-quarters of the mini marshmallows into a heatproof mixing bowl set over a pan of barely simmering water. Add 4 tablespoons of hot water to the bowl then stir continuously with a wooden spoon

until the marshmallows melt and become thick and shiny. Pile the marshmallow into a piping bag fitted with a 1cm round nozzle.

To build the tower, take a dinner plate or a cake stand with a 23cm (9in) base. Pipe a ring of marshmallow about 2cm (1in) from the edge of the plate – this will stick the first layer of doughnuts to the base. Put 11 doughnuts in a ring on top of the mallow, pipe 3 dots of marshmallow into the centre then put 3 doughnuts inside the outer ring. Pipe a blob of marshmallow at the top of where the doughnuts meet. Place 9 doughnuts on top of the first layer, and put 2 doughnuts in the middle, securing with more marshmallow. Continue

to pipe marshmallow into the gaps to secure the doughnuts. Continue this method, putting 7 doughnuts in a ring for the third layer, 5 doughnuts for the fourth layer and 3 doughnuts at the top of the tower, securing with melted marshmallow as you build.

To decorate the tower, fill in any big gaps around the outside of the tower with marshmallow. Dot the remaining mini marshmallows over and allow to set for 5 minutes. Drizzle the melted chocolate all over the tower, making sure all of the doughnuts get a generous helping. Allow the chocolate to just set before presenting to friends to devour – you might need the help of a small knife to help prize the tower apart!

DOUGHNUT SUNDAES

If you want a bit of everything this is the dish for you!

MAKES 6 LARGE OR 30 MINI (SEE PAGE 88) ————————————

100G/4OZ PLAIN FLOUR
1 TSP BAKING POWDER
75G/2½OZ CASTER SUGAR
1 EGG, LIGHTLY BEATEN2 TBSP
SUNFLOWER OIL
85G/3OZ NATURAL YOGURT

To finish
500G TUB CARAMEL ICE CREAM
SHOP-BOUGHT TOFFEE SAUCE, FOR
  DRIZZLING
LARGE HANDFUL SALTED PEANUTS,
  ROUGHLY CHOPPED

Preheat the oven to 180C/350F/ gas 4. Put the flour, baking powder, sugar, egg, oil and yogurt into a mixing bowl and beat until smooth.

Use 2 teaspoons to dollop the mixture into a greased doughnut tin, making sure you don't cover the middle with mixture.

Bake for 10–12 minutes, or until risen and springy to the touch. Leave to cool in the tin for a few minutes, then transfer the doughnuts to a wire rack to cool completely.

Cut the doughnuts in halve and put one half into 6 sundae glasses, add a ball of ice cream and a drizzle of toffee sauce, scatter over some chopped nuts then repeat the layering with the remaining doughnuts halves, a drizzle of sauce, more ice cream and top with a final sprinkling of peanuts. Serve immediately.

ICE-CREAM SANDWICHES

In the south of Italy they pack scoops of gelato into soft, buttery brioche rolls. How about a scoop of your favourite ice cream in a soft, sugary doughnut? Yes please!

MAKES 12

225ML/8FL OZ MILK
50G/2OZ BUTTER, DICED
2 EGGS, LIGHTLY BEATEN
500G/1LB 2OZ STRONG WHITE BREAD
 FLOUR, PLUS EXTRA FOR DUSTING
50G/2OZ CASTER SUGAR
1 X 7G SACHET DRIED FAST-ACTION
 YEAST

To finish
50G/2OZ BUTTER, MELTED
100G/4OZ CASTER SUGAR

For the filling
1 LITRE/1¾ PINTS OF YOUR
 FAVOURITE ICE CREAM

Make up the dough following the method on page 16 (The Classic) to the end of step 4.

Preheat the oven to 180C/350F/ gas 4. Bake the doughnuts for about 12–15 minutes, or until the doughnuts are golden and sound hollow when you tap their underside. Transfer to a wire rack to cool.

Once cool enough to handle, brush the doughnuts with butter then roll in the caster sugar. Put back on the wire rack and leave to cool for another couple of minutes.

While the doughnuts are still a little bit warm, split them almost in half through the centre, tease the 2 halves apart and fill with a scoop of your favourite ice cream. Sandwich together and serve immediately with plenty of napkins.

SUGAR & SPICE

This tear 'n' share bread is perfect for brunch – just let everyone dig in.

MAKES 24

225ML/8FL OZ MILK
50G/2OZ BUTTER, DICED,
  PLUS EXTRA FOR GREASING
2 EGGS, LIGHTLY BEATEN
500G/1LB 2OZ STRONG WHITE BREAD
  FLOUR, PLUS EXTRA FOR DUSTING
50G/2OZ CASTER SUGAR
1 X 7G SACHET DRIED FAST-ACTION
  YEAST
ZEST 1 ORANGE

1 TSP MIXED SPICE
1 TSP GROUND CINNAMON

To finish
140G/5OZ CASTER SUGAR
1½ TSP MIXED SPICE
1½ TSP GROUND CINNAMON
75G/2½OZ BUTTER, MELTED
ICING SUGAR, TO DUST

Make up the dough following the method on page 16 (The Classic) to the end of step 3, adding the orange zest, mixed spice and cinnamon to the other dry ingredients in step 2. Grease a 23cm (9in) springform cake tin with plenty of butter then set aside.

Remove the dough from the bowl and knead briefly on a well-floured work surface to get rid of any air bubbles. Flatten the dough to a 2cm (1in) thickness. Use a 6cm (2½in) round cutter to stamp out the dough or cut it into 24 equal parts with a knife, then shape into neat balls.

Mix the sugar and spices together and put the melted butter in another bowl.

Dip each dough ball into the butter then roll in the sugar/spice mixture. Transfer the balls to the cake tin, leaving a small gap between each ball – you should have about 13 dough balls on the base. Put the remaining balls on top, covering any gaps. Sit the cake tin on a baking tray, loosely cover with a cloth and leave to stand for about 30 minutes, or until doubled in size.

To bake, preheat the oven to 180C/ 350F/gas 4. Bake the doughnut bread for 15 minutes. Remove from the oven, cover loosely with foil then continue to cook for 35 minutes, or until dark brown and crunchy on top. Allow to cool for 5 minutes in the tin. Serve warm dusted with icing sugar.

PUMPKIN PINWHEELS

Spiced, sweet pumpkin pinwheels, sugary and nutty. The perfect doughnut to set you up for an evening of trick or treating.

1 X 425G CAN PUMPKIN PURÉE
125ML/4FL OZ MILK
500G/1LB 2OZ STRONG WHITE BREAD
 FLOUR, PLUS EXTRA FOR DUSTING
1 X 7G SACHET DRIED FAST-ACTION
 YEAST
1 TSP GROUND CINNAMON
1 TSP MIXED SPICE
½ TSP GROUND GINGER
75G/2½OZ DEMERARA SUGAR
SUNFLOWER OIL, FOR GREASING

For the filling
100G/4OZ PECAN NUTS, FINELY
 CHOPPED
100G/4OZ DEMERARA SUGAR
1 TSP GROUND CINNAMON
1 TSP MIXED SPICE
50G/2OZ BUTTER, MELTED

To finish
2 TBSP MAPLE SYRUP

Put the pumpkin purée and milk into a small pan and heat to just below boiling point. Remove from the heat and leave to cool for about 5 minutes until you can comfortably dip your little finger into the liquid.

Put the flour, yeast, spices and sugar into a large mixing bowl and stir to combine, then add a pinch of salt. Make a well in the centre of the flour and gradually stir in the pumpkin mixture to form a very soft, quite sticky dough.

Tip the dough onto a floured work surface. Bring the mixture together,

turning and kneading for 2 minutes, and dusting with flour as required. Place the dough into a lightly greased bowl, cover with a clean cloth and leave to stand in a warm spot until doubled in size – about 1 hour.

Mix together the pecan nuts, sugar and spices and set aside.

Tip out the dough onto a well-floured work surface. Press out to a 1cm (½in) thick, 35cm x 25cm (14in x 10in) rectangle. Brush the surface of the dough with melted butter then sprinkle over the nut mix in an even layer. Starting with the longest

edge that is furthest away from you, carefully roll the dough into a long sausage. Cut the sausage into 12 equal slices with a sharp knife. Transfer the slices, cut side up, to a baking tray lined with baking paper, allowing them just to touch. Loosely cover with a cloth and leave to stand for about 30 minutes.

To bake, preheat the oven to 180C/350F/gas 4. Bake the pinwheels for about 30 minutes. Remove from the oven, brush with maple syrup then return to the oven and continue cooking for 10 minutes, or until golden. Allow to cool for 10 minutes then transfer to a wire rack to cool completely.

DOUBLE CHOCOLATE NESTS

Everything you want for Easter: chocolate dough, thick chocolate ganache
and crisp, sugar-coated eggs. Only thing missing is a handsome Easter bunny!

MAKES 6

225ML/8FL OZ MILK
50G/2OZ BUTTER, DICED
2 EGGS, LIGHTLY BEATEN
500G/1LB 2OZ STRONG WHITE BREAD
 FLOUR, PLUS EXTRA FOR DUSTING
50G/2OZ CASTER SUGAR
1 X 7G SACHET DRIED FAST-ACTION
 YEAST
3 TBSP COCOA POWDER

To finish
150ML/¼ PINT DOUBLE CREAM
1 TBSP GOLDEN SYRUP
140G/5OZ PLAIN CHOCOLATE (70%
 COCOA SOLIDS), ROUGHLY CHOPPED
24 SUGAR-COATED MINI EGGS

Make up the dough following the
method on page 16 (The Classic)
to the end of step 4, adding the
cocoa powder to the rest of the dry
ingredients in step 2.

To make the chocolate ganache
topping, heat the cream and golden
syrup to just below boiling point. Put
the chocolate into a mixing bowl then
pour the hot cream over. Allow to
stand for 5 minutes, then stir until you
have a smooth, thick sauce. Allow to
cool for 30 minutes, or until thick and
spreadable.

Preheat the oven to 180C/350F/
gas 4. Bake the doughnuts for
about 12–15 minutes, or until the
doughnuts are golden and sound
hollow when you tap their underside.
Transfer to a wire rack to cool.

Once the doughnuts are cool, dollop
a tablespoon of the rich chocolate
ganache on top, make a little dip in
the sauce with the back of a spoon,
pop 2 sugar-coated eggs on top of
each and serve.

PASSIONATE PASSION FRUIT

Give me a dozen of these over a dozen red roses any day of the week.
Passionate and edible... perfect!

MAKES 12 ————————————————————————

225ML/8FL OZ MILK
50G/2OZ BUTTER, DICED
2 EGGS, LIGHTLY BEATEN
500G/1LB 2OZ STRONG WHITE BREAD
  FLOUR, PLUS EXTRA FOR DUSTING
50G/2OZ CASTER SUGAR
1 X 7G SACHET DRIED FAST-ACTION
  YEAST

For the filling
200ML/7FL OZ MANGO AND PASSION
  FRUIT SMOOTHIE
3 EGG YOLKS
50G/2OZ CASTER SUGAR
1 TBSP CORNFLOUR
75ML/2½FL OZ DOUBLE CREAM

For the glaze
250G/9OZ ICING SUGAR
2 PASSION FRUIT, PULP ONLY

Make up the dough following the method on page 16 (The Classic) to the end of step 4.

To make the filling, gently heat the mango and passion fruit smoothie until just below boiling point in a small pan. In a large bowl mix the egg yolks, sugar and cornflour until combined. Remove the smoothie from the heat and gradually add to the yolk mixture, stirring all of the time. Pour the mixture back into the pan and cook over a medium heat, stirring continuously for about 5 minutes or until smooth and thick. Remove from

the heat, tip out into a clean bowl, cover the surface with cling film and allow to cool completely.

Preheat the oven to 180C/350F/ gas 4. Bake the doughnuts for about 12–15 minutes, or until the doughnuts are golden and sound hollow when you tap their underside. Transfer to a wire rack to cool.

Use the end of a dessertspoon to make a hole in the side of each doughnut. Wiggle the handle around to create a little space for the passion fruit filling. Whip the cream to soft peaks then

fold through the passionfruit custard. Pile into a piping bag fitted with a 0.5cm round nozzle then squeeze the filling into each of the doughnuts until you can squeeze no more!

To make the glaze, mix the icing sugar with the passion fruit pulp until you have a thick, spreadable mixture – you may need to add a drop of water depending on how juicy your passion fruits are. Slide a baking tray under the wire rack to catch any drips, then spread the glaze over the tops of the doughnuts and allow to set for a few minutes before serving.

SPICED CHRISTMAS RINGS

Find it difficult enough to feed yourself, let alone a Christmas cake?
Why not ditch the cake and make these super-quick and easy Christmas
doughnut rings instead.

MAKES 6 ────────────────────────────────

100G/4OZ PLAIN FLOUR
1 TSP BAKING POWDER
½ TSP ALLSPICE
½ TSP GROUND CINNAMON
¼ TSP GROUND GINGER
75G/2½OZ SOFT DARK BROWN SUGAR
50G/2OZ CURRANTS
25G/1OZ CANDIED PEEL
1 EGG, LIGHTLY BEATEN

2 TBSP SUNFLOWER OIL
100G/4OZ NATURAL YOGURT

For the topping
100G/4OZ ICING SUGAR
¼ TSP MIXED SPICE
1–1½ TBSP BRANDY (OPTIONAL)

Preheat the oven to 180C/350F/
gas 4. Put the flour, baking powder,
spices, sugar, currants, candied peel,
egg, oil and yogurt into a mixing bowl
and beat until smooth.

Use 2 teaspoons to dollop the mixture
into a greased doughnut tin, making
sure you don't cover the middle with
mixture.

Bake for 10–12 minutes, or until risen
and springy to the touch. Leave to
cool in the tin for a few minutes, then
transfer the doughnuts to a wire rack
to cool completely.

Mix the icing sugar, mixed spice and
enough brandy (you can use water if
you prefer) to give a smooth, runny
icing. Slide a piece of baking paper
under the wire rack to catch any drips
then drizzle the doughnuts with the
icing. Allow to set before serving.

CANDY CANES

These are perfect to dunk into a steaming mug of hot chocolate.

225ML/8FL OZ MILK
50G/2OZ BUTTER, DICED
2 EGGS, LIGHTLY BEATEN
500G/1LB 2OZ STRONG WHITE BREAD
  FLOUR, PLUS EXTRA FOR DUSTING
50G/2OZ CASTER SUGAR
1 X 7G SACHET DRIED FAST-ACTION
YEAST

For the topping
400G/14OZ ICING SUGAR
¼ TSP PEPPERMINT ESSENCE OR
  EXTRACT (OPTIONAL)
A FEW DROPS GREEN FOOD COLOURING

To finish
8 (OR 250G) CANDY CANES, CRUSHED

Make up the dough following the method on page 16 (The Classic) to the end of step 3.

Remove the dough from the bowl and knead briefly on a well-floured work surface to get rid of any air bubbles. Flatten the dough to a 2cm (1in) thickness. Use a 7cm (2½in) round cutter to stamp out the dough or cut into 12 equal parts with a knife, then shape into 20cm (8in) long sausages. Transfer to two baking trays lined with baking paper, leaving a 5cm (2in) space between each sausage. Loosely cover with a cloth and leave to stand for about 30 minutes, or until doubled in size.

Preheat the oven to 180C/350F/ gas 4. Bake the doughnuts for 18–20 minutes, or until the doughnuts are golden and sound hollow when you tap their underside. Transfer to a wire rack to cool.

To make the topping, mix the icing sugar, peppermint essence and a few drops of green food colouring with 4–5 tablespoons water, to make a thick but spreadable icing. Use a round-ended knife to spread the doughnut sticks with the icing. Sprinkle with crushed-up candy cane and allow to set before serving with steaming mugs of hot chocolate.

BLUEBERRY CHEESECAKE

I suggest you eat this one with a fork and a bib – the juicy blueberries have a habit of rolling right down your front!

225ML/8FL OZ MILK
50G/2OZ BUTTER, DICED
2 EGGS, LIGHTLY BEATEN
500G/1LB 2OZ STRONG WHITE BREAD
  FLOUR, PLUS EXTRA FOR DUSTING
50G/2OZ CASTER SUGAR
1 X 7G SACHET DRIED FAST-ACTION
  YEAST

For the filling
2 X 300G TUBS CREAM CHEESE
200G/7OZ FAT-FREE GREEK YOGURT
1 TSP VANILLA ESSENCE
85G/3OZ ICING SUGAR
ZEST AND JUICE 1 LEMON
300G/11OZ BLUEBERRIES
2 TSP CORNFLOUR

To finish
3 DIGESTIVE BISCUITS, BASHED TO
  CRUMBS
25G/1OZ BUTTER, MELTED

Make up the dough, following the method on page 16 (The Classic) to the end of step 3.

Remove the dough from the bowl and knead briefly on a well-floured work surface to get rid of any air bubbles. Flatten the dough to a 2cm (1in) thickness. Use a 7cm (3in) round cutter to stamp out the dough or cut into 12 equal parts with a knife, then shape each piece of dough into a 10cm (4in) long sausage shape.

Transfer to two baking trays lined with baking paper, leaving a 5cm (2in) space between each length of dough. Loosely cover with a cloth and leave to stand for about 30 minutes, or until doubled in size.

Preheat the oven to 180C/350F/ gas 4. Bake the doughnuts for about 12–15 minutes, or until the doughnuts are golden and sound hollow when you tap their underside. Transfer to a wire rack to cool completely.

To make the filling, beat the cream cheese, yogurt and vanilla essence with 2 tablespoons of icing sugar and the zest and juice of half the lemon until smooth, then chill until ready to fill your doughnuts.

To make the blueberry sauce, put the blueberries in a pan with the remaining icing sugar and lemon juice and zest. Cook over a medium heat for 5 minutes until most of the blueberries have burst and it looks saucy. Mix the cornflour with 2 teaspoons of water then add to the blueberries. Continue to cook for 2 minutes until thickened and glossy. Remove from the heat and cool.

Split the doughnuts lengthways through the top, being careful not to cut through to the base. Gently prize the sides apart, spoon or pipe in the cream cheese then divide the blueberry sauce between the doughnuts. Mix the digestives with the melted butter and sprinkle over the top of each doughnut before eating.

AFTER-DINNER MINTS

I used to love those little foil-wrapped, crispy mints served after dinner.
These are the doughnut version – soft on the bottom, minty and crisp on
top. With this recipe, you can make 30 mini doughnuts using a doughnut maker
or 6 large doughnuts using a doughnut tin. Whenever you see 'makes 30 mini'
throughout this book, it means that you can use a doughnut maker, if you like.
Just follow the below method alongside the manufacturer's instructions for your
doughnut maker.

MAKES 30 MINI OR 6 LARGE ─────────────────────────────

100G/4OZ PLAIN FLOUR
1 TSP BAKING POWDER
2 TBSP COCOA POWDER
75G/3OZ CASTER SUGAR
1 EGG, LIGHTLY BEATEN
2 TBSP SUNFLOWER OIL
85G/3OZ NATURAL YOGURT

For the topping
100G/4OZ DARK CHOCOLATE (70%
  COCOA SOLIDS)
A FEW DROPS PEPPERMINT ESSENCE
2 TBSP DEMERARA SUGAR

If making 30 mini doughnuts,
using a doughnut maker, read
and familiarise yourself with the
manufacturer's instructions and
preheat as advised.

If you're making 6 large doughnuts,
using a doughnut tin, grease the tin
and preheat the oven to 180C/350F/
gas 4.

Put the flour, baking powder, cocoa,
sugar, egg, oil and yogurt into a
mixing bowl and beat until smooth.

Use 2 teaspoons to carefully spoon the
mixture into the doughnut machine
or the doughnut tin. Resist the urge to
overfill the holes, and make sure you
don't cover the middle with mixture.

Bake the mini doughnuts, in batches,
for 3–4 minutes in the doughnut
maker, or until risen and springy
to the touch. Carefully remove the
doughnuts as they will be very soft at
first – use the handle end of a spoon
to help prise them out. Transfer to a
wire rack to cool completely.

Bake the large doughnuts for 10–12 minutes in the oven, or until risen and springy. Leave to cool in the tin for a few minutes, then transfer the doughnuts to a wire rack to cool completely.

To make the topping, put the chocolate and peppermint essence in a microwaveable bowl and melt the chocolate in bursts of 20 seconds, stirring until it is melted and silky smooth. Allow to cool for 5 minutes.

Stir in the sugar, then use the round end of a knife to cover the tops of the doughnuts with the mixture. Allow the chocolate to go hard before serving.

CHAPTER 5

FANCY

CUSTARD BUÑUELOS

I urge you to wait until your guests arrive before you taste these or you may find yourself with a very full belly and no pud for everyone else! As the saying goes, once you start, you just can't stop.

MAKES 24

85G/3OZ BUTTER, DICED
140G/5OZ PLAIN FLOUR, SIFTED
3 EGGS, LIGHTLY BEATEN

To finish
1 LITRE/1¾ PINTS SUNFLOWER OIL
ICING SUGAR, FOR DUSTING

For the filling
200ML/7FL OZ MILK
3 EGG YOLKS
50G/2OZ CASTER SUGAR
1 TBSP CORNFLOUR
1 VANILLA POD, SEEDS SCRAPED
100ML/3½FL OZ DOUBLE CREAM

First make the filling. Gently heat the milk until just below boiling point. In a separate bowl mix the egg yolks, sugar, cornflour and the vanilla seeds until combined. Remove the milk from the heat and gradually add to the yolk mixture, stirring all the time. Pour the mixture back into the pan and cook over a medium heat for about 5 minutes, stirring continuously, until smooth and thick. Remove from the heat, tip into a bowl, cover the surface with cling film and allow to cool completely.

Put the butter into a medium-sized pan with 225ml (8fl oz) water and heat gently to melt the butter. Once melted, increase the heat and bring to the boil. Remove from the heat, add the flour and beat the mixture with a wooden spoon until you get a smooth, shiny dough that leaves the sides of the pan. Tip into a mixing bowl and allow to cool for 5 minutes.

Gradually add the eggs and continue to beat until you have a smooth dough that falls reluctantly from the spoon.

Pour the oil into a medium-sized, deep saucepan – the oil should be about 5cm (2in) deep – and heat the oil to 180C/350F. Quickly dip 2 teaspoons into the hot oil, then use to drop spoonfuls of dough into the hot oil.

Fry in batches of 2–3, making sure you do not overcrowd the pan. Fry for 3–5 minutes, or until golden and puffed up.

Remove with a slotted spoon and drain on kitchen paper. Continue frying until all of the doughnuts are cooked. Allow to cool completely.

Whip the cream to soft peaks, then fold through the custard. Split the buñuelos open and spoon or pipe the custard into the middle. Serve dusted with icing sugar.

TIRAMISU

Great flavours of a classic pud!

MAKES 6

100G/4OZ PLAIN FLOUR
1 TSP BAKING POWDER
75G/2½OZ SOFT LIGHT BROWN SUGAR
1 TBSP COCOA POWDER
1 TBSP INSTANT COFFEE POWDER
1 EGG, LIGHTLY BEATEN
2 TBSP OIL
75ML/2½FL OZ MILK

For the filling
6 TBSP BRANDY OR COFFEE LIQUEUR
1 TSP INSTANT COFFEE POWDER
140G/5OZ MASCARPONE
1 TBSP ICING SUGAR

Preheat the oven to 180C/350F/ gas 4. Put the flour, baking powder, sugar, cocoa, coffee powder, egg, oil and milk into a mixing bowl and beat until smooth.

Use 2 teaspoons to dollop the mixture into a greased doughnut tin, making sure you don't cover the middle with mixture.

Bake for 10–12 minutes, or until risen and springy to the touch. Leave to cool in the tin for a few minutes, then transfer the doughnuts to a wire rack to cool completely.

Mix the booze of your choice with the coffee powder and stir to dissolve. Split the doughnuts in half horizontally through the centre then drizzle the top and bottom half of each one with half a tablespoon of the coffee mixture.

Beat the mascarpone and icing sugar until really smooth then spread generously over the bottom half of each doughnut, sandwich with the top half and serve immediately or chill until required.

FRITTERS with HONEY-BAKED FIGS

Sweet figs servevd with crisp triangles of dough, dolloped with crème fraîche.

300G/11OZ PLAIN FLOUR, PLUS EXTRA
  FOR DUSTING
3 TSP BAKING POWDER
50G/2OZ CASTER SUGAR
50G/2OZ BUTTER, DICED
175ML/6FL OZ MILK

For the honey-baked figs
25G/1OZ BUTTER, SOFTENED
25G/1OZ CASTER SUGAR
1 TSP GROUND CINNAMON
8 FIGS, HALVED
3 TBSP HONEY

To finish
1 LITRE/1¾ PINTS SUNFLOWER OIL
200G TUB CRÈME FRAÎCHE

Put the plain flour, baking powder and caster sugar into a mixing bowl and stir to combine. Add the diced butter then rub in with your fingertips until the mix resembles fine breadcrumbs.

Gently heat the milk until just warm then add to the dry ingredients and use a round-ended knife to form a soft dough. Tip out onto a lightly floured work surface and knead briefly to make a soft dough.

Add a little more flour to the surface then roll the dough out to form a 20cm x 20cm (8in x 8in)

square. Divide the large square into 4 horizontally, then make 4 cuts vertically to give 16 equal-sized squares. Cut each individual square diagonally to form 2 triangles. Chill for 10 minutes.

Meanwhile, to make the figs, preheat the oven to 200C/400F/gas 6. Mix the butter, sugar and cinnamon until combined. Cut a cross in the figs from their tops halfway down to the base, squeezing the base so that the figs open up a little bit, and transfer to a baking dish. Dot a little of the spiced butter mixture into the centre of each fig, drizzle with the honey then add a couple of tablespoons of water to the dish. Cook for 15–18 minutes, or until the figs are soft and juicy. Allow to cool slightly.

Pour the oil into a medium-sized, deep saucepan – the oil should be about 5cm (2in) deep – and heat the oil to 160C/325F. Carefully lower 3–4 dough triangles at a time into the hot oil and fry for 4–5 minutes, flipping halfway through, until puffed and golden. Remove with a slotted spoon and drain on kitchen paper. Continue frying until all of the fritters are cooked.

Serve 3–4 fritters with a baked fig and a spoon of their syrupy juices, along with a dollop of crème fraîche.

COFFEE & WALNUT PRALINE ÉCLAIRS

Hidden nuggets of crunchy walnut praline in soft coffee cream make these very fancy indeed.

85G/3OZ BUTTER, DICED
140G/5OZ PLAIN FLOUR, SIFTED
3 EGGS, LIGHTLY BEATEN

For the filling
75G/2½OZ WALNUT HALVES, ROUGHLY CHOPPED
75G/2½OZ GRANULATED SUGAR
1 TBSP INSTANT COFFEE POWDER

600ML/1 PINT DOUBLE CREAM
1 TSP VANILLA EXTRACT

For the topping
1 TSP INSTANT COFFEE POWDER
140G/5OZ ICING SUGAR
1 TSP VANILLA EXTRACT

To make the praline, put the roughly chopped walnuts into a small frying pan and cook over a medium heat for 5 minutes, or until fragrant, being careful not to let them burn. Tip in the granulated sugar and cook for a further 3–5 minutes, stirring frequently. Once the sugar melts, stir the nuts to coat them in the caramel. Tip them out onto baking paper lined baking tray and allow to cool completely.

Preheat the oven to 200C/400F/gas 6. Put the butter into a medium-sized pan with 225ml (8fl oz) water and heat gently to melt the butter. Once melted, increase the heat and

bring to the boil. Remove from the heat, add the flour and beat the mixture with a wooden spoon until you get a smooth, shiny dough that leaves the sides of the pan. Tip into a mixing bowl and allow to cool for 5 minutes.

Gradually add the eggs and continue to beat until you have a smooth dough that falls reluctantly from the spoon. Pile into a piping bag fitted with a 1.5cm round nozzle.

Line a couple of baking trays with baking paper, then pipe 10 thick, 12cm (5in) long sausages onto it, using a damp finger to smooth any

peaks in the dough. Bake for 25 minutes, until golden and crisp. Remove from the oven and carefully split in half lengthways.

Place cut side up in pairs, on the baking trays and return to the oven for 5 minutes to dry out and crisp up further. Remove from the oven and transfer to a wire rack to cool completely.

Meanwhile, continue to make the filling. Dissolve the coffee powder in 1 tablespoon of water, then add to the cream and vanilla extract in a large bowl. Whip to soft peaks. Put the praline into a sandwich bag and bash with a rolling pin until finely crushed.

Fold this mixture through the coffee cream. Set aside.

To make the topping, dissolve the coffee in 1 tablespoon of water, then stir into the icing sugar and vanilla extract to make a smooth, thick, spreadable icing. Spread generously over the tops of the éclair halves.

Pile praline coffee cream into a piping bag fitted with a 1cm (½in) round nozzle. Pipe or spoon the filling into the bottom half of the split éclair.

Top with the iced half and eat immediately or chill until ready to serve.

CHAMPAGNE & STRAWBERRIES

Light and crisp choux pastry rings, oven baked and filled with fresh strawberries and champagne cream. Flex those pinkies for these posh treats!

MAKES 10

85G/3OZ BUTTER, DICED
140G/5OZ PLAIN FLOUR, SIFTED
3 EGGS, LIGHTLY BEATEN

For the filling
200G/7OZ STRAWBERRIES, HULLED
 AND ROUGHLY CHOPPED

4 TBSP CHAMPAGNE
2 TBSP ICING SUGAR, PLUS EXTRA
 FOR DUSTING
300ML/½ PINT DOUBLE CREAM

Preheat the oven to 200C/400F/ gas 6. Line 2 baking trays with baking paper, then draw 5 circles on each using a 9cm (4in) round cutter as a guide. Flip the paper over, so you don't get pencil on your rings!

Put the butter into a medium-sized pan with 225ml (8fl oz) water and heat gently to melt the butter. Once melted, increase the heat and bring to the boil. Remove from the heat, add the flour and beat the mixture with a wooden spoon until you get a smooth, shiny dough that leaves the sides of the pan. Tip into a mixing bowl and allow to cool for 5 minutes.

Gradually add the eggs and continue to beat until you have a smooth dough that falls reluctantly from the spoon.

Pile into a piping bag fitted with a 1.5cm star nozzle.

Pipe 10 thick rings on the inside edge of the circles you have drawn on the paper. Bake for 25 minutes, until golden and crisp. Remove from the oven and carefully split in half through the centre. Place cut side up in pairs on the baking trays and return to the oven for 5 minutes to dry out and crisp up further.

Remove from the oven, transfer to a wire rack and allow to cool completely.

To make the filling, put the strawberries in a bowl with a tablespoon of champagne and a tablespoon of icing sugar, stir, and allow to stand for 5 minutes. Meanwhile, put the cream into a large mixing bowl with the remaining champagne and icing sugar and whip it to soft peaks.

Gently fold the strawberries and any juices through the cream.

Use a couple of teaspoons to fill the choux rings with the champagne strawberries and cream.

Serve dusted with icing sugar – you may wish to use a little fork to eat these as they are so posh!

GOAT'S CHEESE PUFFS

Serve with sticky onion chutney and a salad and serve as a light lunch.

MAKES 24 ───────────────────────────────────────

85G/3OZ BUTTER, DICED
140G/5OZ PLAIN FLOUR, SIFTED
3 EGGS, LIGHTLY BEATEN

For the filling
200G/7OZ SOFT RINDLESS GOAT'S
  CHEESE

100ML/4FL OZ DOUBLE CREAM
2 TBSP FINELY CHOPPED CHIVES

To finish
1 LITRE/1¾ PINTS SUNFLOWER OIL
YOUR FAVOURITE ONION CHUTNEY

Put the butter into a medium-sized pan with 225ml (8fl oz) water and heat gently to melt the butter. Once melted, increase the heat and bring to the boil. Remove from the heat, add the flour and beat the mixture with a wooden spoon until you get a smooth, shiny dough that leaves the sides of the pan. Tip into a mixing bowl and allow to cool for 5 minutes.

Meanwhile, make the filling. Put the goat's cheese into a mixing bowl and beat until really smooth, then gradually stir in the cream until thick and smooth. Add the chives and plenty of black pepper then stir to combine. Chill until required.

Gradually add the eggs to the cooled dough and continue to beat until you have a smooth dough that falls reluctantly from the spoon.

Pour the oil into a medium-sized, deep saucepan – the oil should be about 5cm (2in) deep – and heat the oil to 180C/350F.

Quickly dip 2 teaspoons into the hot oil, then use to drop heaped spoonfuls of dough into the oil, one at a time.

Fry in batches of 2–3, making sure you do not overcrowd the pan. Fry for 3–5 minutes, or until golden and puffed up. Remove with a slotted spoon and drain on kitchen paper. Continue frying until all of the doughnuts are cooked. Allow to cool completely.

Split the puffs open and spoon the creamy goat's cheese filling into the middle. Serve with a dollop of your favourite chutney.

PARMESAN & PARMA HAM BITES

These are the perfect nibbles to serve with drinks. A wonderful cross between a croquette and a doughnut. Crunchy, salty and totally moreish, especially when served with the popular Italian aperitivo, Aperol Spritz.

MAKES 24 ─────────────────────────────

85G/3OZ BUTTER, DICED
140G/5OZ PLAIN FLOUR, SIFTED
3 EGGS, LIGHTLY BEATEN
6 SLICES PARMA HAM, VERY FINELY
  CHOPPED

25G/1OZ PARMESAN, FINELY GRATED
100G/4OZ POLENTA
1 LITRE/1¾ PINTS SUNFLOWER OIL

Put the butter into a medium-sized pan with 225ml (8fl oz) water and heat gently to melt the butter. Once melted, increase the heat and bring to the boil.

Remove from the heat, add the flour and beat the mixture with a wooden spoon until you get a smooth, shiny dough that leaves the sides of the pan. Tip into a mixing bowl and allow to cool for 5 minutes.

Gradually add the eggs and continue to beat until you have a smooth dough that falls reluctantly from the spoon. Stir in the Parma ham and three-quarters of the grated Parmesan. Put the polenta and remaining Parmesan into a baking dish with some black pepper.

Dollop dessertspoonfuls of the dough into the dish, one at a time, and coat each in the polenta mix.

Pour the oil into a medium-sized, deep saucepan – the oil should be about 5cm (2in) deep – and heat the oil to 180C/350F. Drop the coated dough balls into the hot oil, one at a time. Fry in batches of 3–4, making sure you do not overcrowd the pan. Fry for 3–5 minutes, or until golden and puffed up. Remove with a slotted spoon and drain on kitchen paper. Continue frying until all of the doughnuts are cooked. Allow to cool. Serve at room temperature with drinks.

CHOCOLATE **TRIFLE**

Chocolate, chocolate and more chocolate; so easy yet so impressive.

100G/4OZ PLAIN FLOUR
1 TSP BAKING POWDER
2 TBSP COCOA POWDER
75G/2½OZ DARK SOFT BROWN SUGAR
1 EGG, LIGHTLY BEATEN
2 TBSP SUNFLOWER OIL, PLUS EXTRA
 FOR GREASING
100G/4OZ LOW-FAT NATURAL YOGURT

For the filling
100G/4OZ DARK CHOCOLATE (70%
 COCOA SOLIDS), ROUGHLY CHOPPED
500ML TUB READY-MADE CUSTARD
6 TBSP CHOCOLATE LIQUEUR, OR YOUR
 FAVOURITE TIPPLE
300G/11OZ FROZEN MIXED BERRIES,
DEFROSTED

To finish
300ML/11FL OZ DOUBLE CREAM

Preheat the oven to 180C/350F/ gas 4. Put the flour, baking powder, cocoa, sugar, egg, oil and yogurt into a mixing bowl and beat until smooth.

Use 2 teaspoons to dollop the mixture into a greased doughnut tin, making sure you don't cover the middles with mixture.

Bake for 10–12 minutes, or until risen and springy to the touch. Leave to cool in the tin for a few minutes, then transfer the doughnuts to a wire rack to cool completely.

Heat the chocolate and custard in a small pan over a low heat, stirring until the chocolate has melted, making sure the mixture does not boil. Remove from the heat, cover the surface of the custard with cling film and allow to cool completely.

Put a doughnut into the bases of 6 x 250ml (9fl oz) serving dishes, spoon over a tablespoon of liqueur and allow it to soak in. Top with the berries and any juices and leave to stand for 5 minutes.

Divide the custard between the dishes, and chill until required. Just before serving, lightly whip the cream until it just holds its shape, then dollop a little on top of each trifle.

DILL & SMOKED SALMON

Make mini versions of these bakes using a doughnut maker, for a cute canapé.

MAKES 6 LARGE OR 30 MINI (SEE PAGE 88)

100G/4OZ PLAIN FLOUR
1 TSP BAKING POWDER
25G/1OZ CASTER SUGAR
1 TSP SALT
1 EGG, LIGHTLY BEATEN
2 TBSP SUNFLOWER OIL
100G/4OZ LOW-FAT NATURAL YOGURT
1½ TBSP FINELY CHOPPED DILL

For the filling
200G TUB CREAM CHEESE
ZEST AND JUICE 1 LEMON
2 SPRING ONIONS, FINELY CHOPPED
1 TBSP CAPERS, DRAINED AND FINELY
 CHOPPED
1 TBSP FINELY CHOPPED DILL
150G PACK SMOKED SALMON, SLICED
 INTO SMALL PIECES

Preheat the oven to 180C/350F/ gas 4. Put the flour, baking powder, sugar, salt, egg, oil and yogurt into a mixing bowl and beat until smooth, then gently fold through the dill.

Use 2 teaspoons to dollop the mixture into a greased doughnut tin, making sure you don't cover the middles with mixture.

Bake for 10–12 minutes, or until risen and springy to the touch. Leave to cool in the tin for a few minutes, then transfer the doughnuts to a wire rack to cool completely.

To make the filling, put the cream cheese into a large mixing bowl and beat with a wooden spoon until smooth. Add the lemon zest and juice, spring onions, capers and dill with lots of seasoning and beat until well combined.

Split each doughnut through the centre, spread a teaspoon full of the cream cheese mixture over the bottom half of the doughnut, top with smoked salmon and sandwich with the top of the doughnut. Serve immediately, or chill until required.

CHAPTER 6

VIRTUOUS

DARK CHOCOLATE & BEETROOT

Deliciously dense, chocolatey, dairy-free doughnuts. Grated beetroot adds a subtle sweetness and the wholemeal flour will help take the guilt away when you eat all six yourself…

MAKES 6

100G/4OZ WHOLEMEAL FLOUR
1 TSP BAKING POWDER
1 TBSP COCOA POWDER,
 PLUS EXTRA FOR DUSTING
75G/2½OZ SOFT LIGHT BROWN SUGAR
1 SMALL RAW BEETROOT (ABOUT
 50G/2OZ), PEELED AND GRATED
1 TSP VANILLA EXTRACT

2 TBSP SUNFLOWER OIL, PLUS EXTRA
 FOR GREASING
85G/3OZ SOYA YOGURT
1 EGG, LIGHTLY BEATEN
85G/3OZ DAIRY-FREE PLAIN CHOCOLATE
 (70% COCOA SOLIDS), MELTED AND
 COOLED

Preheat the oven to 180C/350F/ gas 4. Put the flour, baking powder, cocoa, sugar, beetroot, vanilla, oil, yogurt and egg into a mixing bowl and beat until smooth. Stir in the cooled melted chocolate and beat again until incorporated.

Use 2 teaspoons to dollop the mixture into a greased doughnut tin, making sure you don't cover the middle with mixture.

Bake for 10–12 minutes, or until risen and springy to the touch. Leave to cool in the tin for a few minutes, then transfer the doughnuts to a wire rack to cool completely. Dust with cocoa before serving.

CARROT CAKE

Spiced, sweet, super-moist, wholemeal doughnuts with cream cheese frosting –
a classic combination.

MAKES 6

100G/4OZ WHOLEMEAL FLOUR
1 TSP BAKING POWDER
1 TSP GROUND CINNAMON
½ TSP MIXED SPICE
75G/2½OZ SOFT LIGHT BROWN SUGAR
50G/2OZ GRATED CARROT (ABOUT 1
  SMALL CARROT)
25G/1OZ SULTANAS

2 TBSP SUNFLOWER OIL, PLUS EXTRA
  FOR GREASING
1 EGG, LIGHTLY BEATEN
85G/3OZ SOYA YOGURT

For the topping
100G/4OZ CREAM CHEESE, SOFTENED
2 TBSP ICING SUGAR
GROUND CINNAMON, FOR DUSTING

Preheat the oven to 180C/350F/
gas 4. Put the flour, baking powder,
spices, sugar, carrot, sultanas, oil, egg
and yogurt into a mixing bowl and
beat until smooth.

Use 2 teaspoons to dollop the mixture
into a greased doughnut tin, making
sure you don't cover the middle with
mixture.

Bake for 12–15 minutes, or until risen
and springy to the touch. Leave to

cool in the tin for a few minutes, then
transfer the doughnuts to a wire rack
to cool completely.

To make the topping, beat the cream
cheese with the icing sugar until
smooth. Spread over the top of the
doughnuts and sprinkle with a little
cinnamon before eating.

BANANA & TOASTED COCONUT

Banana and coconut are a winning combo in these gluten- and dairy-free treats.

MAKES 6

75G/2½OZ DESICCATED COCONUT
100G/4OZ GLUTEN-FREE SELF-RAISING
 FLOUR
75G/2½OZ SOFT LIGHT BROWN SUGAR
2 SMALL RIPE BANANAS, MASHED
1 EGG, LIGHTLY BEATEN

2 TBSP SUNFLOWER OIL, PLUS EXTRA
 FOR GREASING
GOOD GRATING FRESH NUTMEG

To finish
3 TBSP APRICOT JAM

Preheat the oven to 180C/350F/ gas 4. Put the coconut on a baking tray and cook for 5 minutes, stirring halfway through, until golden and toasted. Remove from the oven and allow to cool.

Put the flour, 2 tablespoons of the roasted coconut, sugar, mashed banana, egg and oil into a mixing bowl, add a grating of nutmeg and beat until smooth.

Use 2 teaspoons to dollop the mixture into a greased doughnut tin, making sure you don't cover the middle with mixture.

Bake for 12–15 minutes, or until risen and springy to the touch. Leave to cool in the tin for a few minutes then transfer the doughnuts to a wire rack to cool completely.

To finish, loosen the apricot jam with a teaspoon of boiled water then brush all over the doughnuts. Drop the doughnuts into the remaining toasted coconut and coat, to finish.

CORN & CHILLI

Vegan, gluten-free doughnuts made with fiery, green chillies and sweetcorn, topped with a fresh avocado and tomato salsa – just serve with cold cervezas…

MAKES 6

50G/2OZ FINE POLENTA OR CORNMEAL

50G/2OZ GLUTEN-FREE SELF-RAISING FLOUR

1 TSP GLUTEN-FREE BAKING POWDER

25G/1OZ SOFT LIGHT BROWN SUGAR

1 X 198G CAN SWEETCORN, DRAINED

2 TBSP SUNFLOWER OIL, PLUS EXTRA FOR GREASING

85G/3OZ SOYA YOGURT

2 SPRING ONIONS, FINELY CHOPPED

2 GREEN CHILLIES, FINELY CHOPPED

To finish

100G/4OZ CHERRY TOMATOES, ROUGHLY CHOPPED

3 SPRING ONIONS, ROUGHLY CHOPPED

1 AVOCADO, PEELED, STONED AND ROUGHLY CHOPPED

HANDFUL CORIANDER, ROUGHLY CHOPPED

JUICE ½ LIME

Preheat the oven to 180C/350F/gas 4. Put the polenta, flour, baking powder and sugar into a large mixing bowl and stir to combine.

Put two-thirds of the can of sweetcorn, the oil and yogurt into the bowl of a food processor and whizz until a purée-like consistency. Stir in the remaining sweetcorn, the spring onions and chillies then add the mixture to the dry ingredients and stir to combine.

Use 2 teaspoons to dollop the mixture into a greased doughnut tin, making sure you don't cover the middle with mixture.

Bake for 18–20 minutes, or until light golden and a little crisp on the surface. Leave to cool in the tin for a few minutes, then run a knife round the edge of the doughnuts. Turn the pan over onto a wire rack, give it a bang to release the doughnuts, then leave them to cool.

To finish, make a quick salsa by mixing the tomatoes, spring onions, avocado and coriander with the lime juice and some salt and pepper. Serve with the corn and chilli doughnuts. Or you can cheat and buy a shop-bought salsa, if you prefer.

MEXICAN CHOCOLATE

A hint of spice and a kick of chilli make these gluten- and dairy-free treats stand out from the crowd.

MAKES 6 ───────────────────────────────

100G/4OZ GLUTEN-FREE SELF-RAISING
  FLOUR
1 TSP MIXED SPICE
1 TSP GROUND CINNAMON
¼ TSP HOT CHILLI POWDER
75G/2½OZ SOFT DARK BROWN SUGAR
2 TBSP SUNFLOWER OIL
1 EGG, LIGHTLY BEATEN
85G/3OZ SOYA YOGURT

75G/2½OZ DAIRY-FREE CHOCOLATE,
  MELTED AND COOLED

To finish
50G/2OZ DAIRY-FREE CHOCOLATE,
  MELTED
¼ TSP CHILLI FLAKES (OPTIONAL)

Preheat the oven to 180C/350F/ gas 4. Put the flour, spices, sugar, oil, egg and yogurt into a mixing bowl, add the melted chocolate and beat until smooth.

Use 2 teaspoons to dollop the mixture into a greased doughnut tin, making sure you don't cover the middle with mixture.

Bake for 10–12 minutes, or until risen and springy to the touch. Leave to cool in the tin for a few minutes, then transfer the doughnuts to a wire rack to cool completely.

Drizzle the doughnuts with melted chocolate and a sprinkling of chilli flakes, if you like, before serving.

BERRIES, SEEDS & RYE

Eat one for breakfast and it'll satisfy you until lunch.

MAKES 6

450G/1LB RYE FLOUR, PLUS EXTRA
  FOR DUSTING
1 X 7G SACHET DRIED FAST-ACTION
  YEAST
50G/2OZ SOFT LIGHT BROWN SUGAR

75G/2½OZ MIXED SEEDS
150G PACK MIXED DRIED BERRIES
SUNFLOWER OIL, FOR GREASING

Put the flour, yeast, sugar, seeds and dried berries into a large mixing bowl and stir to combine, then add a pinch of salt. Make a well in the centre of the flour and add 280–325ml (10–11fl oz) warm water to form a dough– don't add all the water at once as you may need a little more, or less, than stated.

Tip the dough onto a lightly floured work surface and knead for 10 minutes, or until you have a soft dough – it won't be as elastic as normal dough because rye flour contains less gluten. Place the dough into a lightly greased bowl, cover with a clean cloth and leave to stand in a warm spot until doubled in size – about 1 hour should do it.

Remove the dough from the bowl and knead briefly on a lightly floured work surface to get rid of any air bubbles. Flatten the dough to a 2cm (1in) thickness. Use a 7cm (3in) round cutter to stamp out the dough, or cut into 12 equal parts using a knife, then shape into neat balls. Transfer to two baking trays lined with baking paper, leaving a 5cm (2in) space between each ball. Loosely cover with a cloth and leave to stand for about 30 minutes, or until doubled in size.

Preheat the oven to 180C/350F/ gas 4. Bake the doughnuts for about 15–18 minutes, or until the doughnuts are golden and sound hollow when you tap their underside. Transfer to a wire rack to cool. Split and serve with butter and honey for breakfast.

LEMON & POPPY SEED

The perfect gluten- and dairy-free breakfast on the go ...

MAKES 6 LARGE OR 30 MINI (SEE PAGE 88)

85G/3OZ GLUTEN-FREE SELF-RAISING
  FLOUR
25G/1OZ GROUND ALMONDS
1 TBSP POPPY SEEDS
75G/2½OZ CASTER SUGAR
ZEST 2 LEMONS
2 TBSP SUNFLOWER OIL
1 EGG, LIGHTLY BEATEN
85G/3OZ SOYA YOGURT

For the topping
100G/4OZ ICING SUGAR
1–2 TBSP LEMON JUICE
COUPLE DROPS YELLOW FOOD
  COLOURING

Preheat the oven to 180C/350F/ gas 4. Put the flour, ground almonds, poppy seeds, sugar, lemon zest, oil, egg and yogurt into a mixing bowl and beat until smooth.

Use 2 teaspoons to dollop the mixture into a greased doughnut tin, making sure you don't cover the middle with mixture.

Bake for 12–15 minutes, or until risen and springy to the touch. Leave to cool in the tin for a few minutes, then transfer the doughnuts to a wire rack to cool completely.

To make the topping, mix the icing sugar with enough lemon juice to make a smooth, thick, runny icing. Add a couple of drops of yellow food colouring. Slide a tray under the wire rack to catch any drips then drizzle each of the doughnuts with a little icing. Allow to set before eating.

DELICIOUS DATE

Sticky, rich and satisfying, these doughnuts taste delicious with a wedge of strong cheese. Using agave syrup makes them vegan, but you can always use honey instead.

MAKES 8 ——————————————————————————————

125G/4½OZ READY-TO-EAT DATES, ROUGHLY CHOPPED

3 TBSP AGAVE SYRUP OR RUNNY HONEY

500G/1LB 2OZ WHOLEMEAL FLOUR, PLUS EXTRA FOR DUSTING

1 X 7G SACHET DRIED FAST-ACTION YEAST

SUNFLOWER OIL, FOR GREASING

To finish

2 TBSP AGAVE SYRUP OR RUNNY HONEY

Put the dates and agave in a small pan with 325ml (11fl oz) water. Heat to just below boiling point. Remove from the heat and use a potato masher to break down the dates. Leave to cool for 5 minutes until you can comfortably dip your little finger into the liquid.

Put the flour and yeast into a large mixing bowl and stir to combine, then add a pinch of salt. Make a well in the centre of the flour and gradually stir in the date mixture to form a soft, slightly sticky dough.

Tip the dough onto a lightly floured work surface and knead for 10 minutes, or until you have a soft

dough – it won't be smooth, but should be elastic. Place the dough into a lightly greased bowl, cover with a clean cloth and leave to stand in a warm spot until doubled in size – about 1 hour should do it.

Remove the dough from the bowl and knead briefly on a lightly floured work surface to get rid of any air bubbles. Flatten the dough to a 1cm (½in) thickness. Use a 10cm (4in) round cutter to stamp out the dough, or cut into 8 equal parts using a knife, then shape into neat balls. Use a 4cm (2in) round cutter to form a hole in the centre of each doughnut, or plunge the handle of a wooden spoon into a bag of flour and make a 4cm

(2in) wide hole in the centre of each doughnut. Transfer to two baking trays lined with baking paper, leaving a 5cm (2in) space between each ring. Loosely cover with a cloth and leave to stand for about 30 minutes, or until doubled in size.

Preheat the oven to 180C/350F/ gas 4. Bake the doughnuts for about 15–18 minutes, or until the doughnuts are golden and sound hollow when you tap their underside. Transfer to a wire rack to cool.

Brush the doughnuts with agave while they are still slightly warm. Enjoy with a wedge of cheese and your favourite pickle.

GINGER & PEAR

Gluten-free and fruity, these pear doughnuts are complimented beautifully by this gingery icing.

MAKES 6 ——————————————————————————————

1 RIPE PEAR, CORED
85G/3OZ GLUTEN-FREE SELF-RAISING
 FLOUR
25G/1OZ GROUND ALMONDS
75G/2½OZ SOFT DARK BROWN SUGAR
½ TSP GROUND GINGER
2 TBSP SUNFLOWER OIL, PLUS EXTRA
 FOR GREASING
1 EGG, LIGHTLY BEATEN

½ STEM GINGER BALL IN SYRUP,
 DRAINED AND FINELY CHOPPED

For the topping
100G/4OZ ICING SUGAR
1–2 TBSP SYRUP FROM THE STEM
 GINGER JAR
1 BALL STEM GINGER, FINELY CHOPPED

Preheat the oven to 180C/350F/ gas 4. Grate the pear into a large mixing bowl, catching any juices as you go. Add the flour, ground almonds, sugar, ground ginger, oil, egg and chopped stem ginger and beat until smooth.

Use 2 teaspoons to dollop the mixture into a greased doughnut tin, making sure you don't cover the middle with mixture.

Bake for 12–15 minutes, or until risen and springy to the touch. Leave to cool in the tin for a few minutes, then transfer the doughnuts to a wire rack to cool completely.

To make the topping, mix the icing sugar with enough ginger syrup to make a smooth, thick, runny icing. You may have to add a drop of water to help it along. Slide a baking tray under the wire rack to catch any drips then drizzle each of the doughnuts with a little icing. Dot some chopped stem ginger over each one and allow to set before eating.

JUST VANILLA

Simple and delicious, these gluten-free, dairy-free vanilla doughnut cakes are suitable for any occasion – from breakfast through to dessert.

MAKES 6 LARGE OR 30 MINI (SEE PAGE 88)

100G/4OZ GLUTEN-FREE SELF-RAISING FLOUR
75G/2½OZ CASTER SUGAR
1 EGG, LIGHTLY BEATEN
2 TBSP SUNFLOWER OIL, PLUS EXTRA FOR GREASING
75ML/2½FL OZ SOYA MILK

1 TSP VANILLA EXTRACT

For the topping
200G/7OZ ICING SUGAR
1 TSP VANILLA EXTRACT

Preheat the oven to 180C/350F/ gas 4. Put the flour, baking powder, egg, oil, milk and vanilla into a mixing bowl and beat until smooth.

Use 2 teaspoons to dollop the mixture into a greased doughnut tin, making sure you don't cover the middle with mixture.

Bake for 10–12 minutes, or until risen and springy to the touch. Leave to cool in the tin for a few minutes, then transfer the doughnuts to a wire rack to cool completely.

Set a large heatproof bowl over a pan of barely simmering water, add the icing sugar, vanilla extract and 2½ tablespoons water and stir until the topping is smooth. Slide a baking tray under the wire rack to catch any drips then dip each doughnut into the icing to coat, putting them back on the wire rack to set before eating.

INDEX

THANK YOUS

Thank you to Random House, particularly Laura Higginson for asking me to come on board with this project and for making it such a fun process. William Reavell for the lovely pictures and the brilliant shoot days. Georgia Vaux for the beautiful book design and Jo Harris for the gorgeous prop styling. Kat and Alex for their help on the shoots. BdL, Daisy A and Catherine Williams for your beady eyes and attention to detail. A very special thank you to everyone who has eaten the doughnuts in the book and given me such brilliant feedback, especially Jean who has been force-fed daily and has had to share her home with over 60 varieties of doughnut!

10 9 8 7 6 5 4 3 2 1

PUBLISHED IN 2013 BY EBURY PRESS, AN IMPRINT OF EBURY PUBLISHING. A RANDOM HOUSE GROUP COMPANY.

TEXT BY ROSIE REYNOLDS © EBURY PUBLISHING 2013
ROSIE REYNOLDS HAS ASSERTED HER RIGHT TO BE IDENTIFIED AS THE AUTHOR OF THIS WORK IN ACCORDANCE WITH THE COPYRIGHT, DESIGNS AND PATENTS ACT 1988

PHOTOGRAPHY BY WILLIAM REAVELL © EBURY PUBLISHING 2013
DESIGN BY GEORGIA VAUX © EBURY PUBLISHING 2013

MIX
Paper from
responsible sources
FSC
www.fsc.org   FSC® C008047

THE RANDOM HOUSE GROUP LIMITED REG. NO. 954009 ADDRESSES FOR COMPANIES WITHIN THE RANDOM HOUSE GROUP CAN BE FOUND AT
WWW.RANDOMHOUSE.CO.UK
A CIP CATALOGUE RECORD FOR THIS BOOK IS AVAILABLE FROM THE BRITISH LIBRARY.

ISBN: 978 0 09 195727 8

THE RANDOM HOUSE GROUP LIMITED SUPPORTS THE FOREST STEWARDSHIP COUNCIL® (FSC®), THE LEADING INTERNATIONAL FOREST-CERTIFICATION ORGANISATION. OUR BOOKS CARRYING THE FSC LABEL ARE PRINTED ON FSC®-CERTIFIED PAPER. FSC IS THE ONLY FOREST-CERTIFICATION SCHEME SUPPORTED BY THE LEADING ENVIRONMENTAL ORGANISATIONS, INCLUDING GREENPEACE. OUR PAPER PROCUREMENT POLICY CAN BE FOUND AT WWW.RANDOMHOUSE.CO.UK/ ENVIRONMENT

COMMISSIONING EDITOR: LAURA HIGGINSON
PRODUCTION: LUCY HARRISON
COLOUR ORIGINATION BY TAG: RESPONSE, UK.
PRINTED AND BOUND IN CHINA BY C&C OFFSET PRINTING CO., LTD

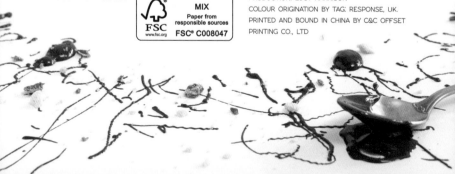